6-30-18

Dear Catherine,

I still treasure the gold cross you gave me, and the "Joan of Arc" silver spoon handle that hangs on my key chain.

You are always in my prayers,

Joan Nedeau

Tenderwise
...Rediscovering Life's Sweet Spots

by

Joan Irgens Nedeau

DORRANCE
PUBLISHING CO
EST. 1920
PITTSBURGH, PENNSYLVANIA 15238

Dorrance Publishing Co
585 Alpha Drive
Suite 103
Pittsburgh, PA 15238
Visit our website at *www.dorrancebookstore.com*

ISBN: 978-1-4809-2463-5
eISBN: 978-1-4809-2233-4

Chapter 1

Liz McKenna walked down 42nd Street from Tudor City into Manhattan's morning rush hour. Her slender figure moved with an energy that belied her seventy years. The sun was out, the air was crisp and the sidewalks to Grand Central Station tilted downhill, giving thrust to her steps. Grand Central Station...well named. It hadn't been long since her return to New York that she realized the grand old station was still proving a center point of her existence in spite of nearly fifty years away from the big city. Confidently present, it stands as a symbol of ageless beauty, inspiring endurance, providing a converging structure for a daily pandemoneous influx of tourists and commuters. Liz was on her way to pick up a Metro Card insuring her transit on buses and the subway for the week for "only twenty dollars. Cheaper than gas," she mused when she remembered what she used to spend maintaining her little Cooper in Minnesota. As impractical as it may seem, even to herself, the other reason for weekly visits to the Station was her passion for fresh bread luring her to the Zoro Bakery at the Market on the main floor. "You walk all the way to Grand Central for bread!" was a familiar response.

When Liz was ten, her father had taken her to Grand Central Station. Its interior's hulk even now sparks youthful recollections for instance, that of "the blue balloon that got away." After a tour of the New York Stock Exchange on Family Day at his work, her father surprised her with a beautiful blue balloon to take home. However, as helium does when unrestrained, her balloon took off as they were walking up one of the huge stairways. Horrified, Liz watched it float up and up, until it settled on a huge marble beam just over their heads. Her precious daddy worked himself onto one of those marble stair bannisters and managed to touch the end of the string just enough to retrieve it from overhead.

Now, back in the city, memories are triggered often, and in recall of the balloon event, even the dialogue remains intact. Her father jumped precariously down to the steps where she stood watching and, regaining his balance, brought her balloon to her, extending the cord first, while directing, "Now, wrap this around your finger and don't let it go." A stranger, a man rushing by, who obviously caught the gist of events, and Liz assumed, for whatever reason, perhaps "admiring my father's patient act of heroism," yelled as he rushed passed, "Wrap it around her neck!" Ugh! New Yorkers are so crass! And then she corrected, "Spontaneous. Hilarious," she continued. "Very funny," she discovered pondering the comparisons of humor The Midwest exudes a more thoughtful and subtle humor. After being raised in New York she decided timing was everything for comedic value on the East Coast. The quickness of retort added the punch. She decided quick wit was perhaps brought on by diverse cultures reflecting off one another in constant interaction, which spills out into hilarious human comedy which one must grasp immediately or risk losing the impact. Thus the balloon incident, "did not cause a childhood trauma nor turn me against balloons," she would assure listeners later in the story. For this reason her enjoyment in sharing the story always included the man's witty sarcasm that, she reasoned, bonded him with her father's dilemma.

"All grown up and taller than her earliest memories," she would muse. "But never to be tall enough to reach, nor skilled enough to wrap my imagination around the grandeur of this magnificent structure that remains a hub anchoring my daily experience." The magnificent heights of its ceilings reigning over arched windows, curved stairways rising into an array of carved marble entrees. She couldn't remember when she began to use its landmark to measure the distance of her morning walk. If she could reach the Station without pulling back her pace, she felt she had fulfilled her endurance goal for the day. Liz was startled suddenly as a women, bent against the crowd jostled her. Irritated, but undaunted, Liz continued her pace, adjusting her scarf against a sudden gust of wind.

As she came up to the corner on Lexington Avenue a swell of sound grew with the steady emergence of commuters from the subways. This sound of mass emergence from the deep into daylight sparked images of herself in her twenties when she commuted daily from the Bronx to work.in Manhattan's Midtown. Along with congestion, still alive in her memories were the shattering sound and dusty speed drafts of approaching trains, amplified by wheels grinding as they were braked against metal tracks. As also, the musty smells of sweat mixed with spicy aromas on clothing and people's breaths, all part of a system that seemed to, and still does, thrive on challenge and paradox, both of which, she was convinced, tested the full range of a person's character and emotions.

Subways spun out an array of human drama every day! If you travel underground often, your senses are primed, aware of the dense din of activity all around you, yet coupled simultaneously with caution to remain safely disengaged. The paradox is in the stories of human interaction. The same man who might inflict a body blow to you in an attempt to fit himself into a subway car before the door closed, might be the same benevolent being that stops his race to the turnstiles to assist you in extracting a Metro Card from the money machines. It is so spontaneous, expresses itself freely and graciously thus seemingly learned behavior of those who spend half their lives underground...the person not even hesitating long enough to be thanked.

Liz enjoyed telling "subway stories" to friends in Minnesota, probably because they sound strange to anyone who hasn't lived the reality. One of her favorites played out on Liz's morning commute. A woman attempted to disembark at her station only to find herself hampered by a tug on her long scarf. She turned to the man next to her and saw that the fringe on her scarf was caught in the zipper of his jacket! Liz remembers her amusement when, later, she related the dismay and frustration of the two people involved. The frantic woman kept yanking her scarf and yelling at the man, "This is my stop!" And he, in desperation, began pulling the fringe in all directions and, with his voice rising, yelling, "I'm trying, lady! I'm trying!" Seeing the crisis, a fellow traveler threw himself against the advance of the closing door giving just enough time for the scarf to break free from the last ditch thrust of team effort, allowing the woman the needed momentum to hurl herself out, and upright, onto the platform. The air, that an instant before, bristled with urgency, settled as everything returned to normal. Passengers resumed their previous positions and conversations, sparing the poor guy in the jacket who, free from further hysterical harassment, sulked in silence.

When sharing stories, Liz did not claim all human oddities occurred just in the confines of New York City. However, after observing residents of cities as opposed to her lived suburban experience, she was convinced the former challenges our perspectives on human resilience. On one of her excursions crosstown she came upon a " bag lady" enjoying a cup of hot coffee in the morning sun, reading the newspaper, no doubt, retrieved from the trash barrel, sitting relaxed on stone steps like a suburban housewife after the kids have left for school, enjoying "free time" while catching up on the latest news. Common, too, is the early morning whir and nerve wracking clank of trucks picking up or delivering. Common is the buzz of power cleaners against old brick buildings, or the shrill of the fire engines bleating their way through congested traffic.

There were times when the daily onslaught of noise irritated her. Eventually, however, Liz began to devise solutions to minimize the effects. When she grew tired of the clash and cymbals of daily crowd muster she turned into a store and continued her browsing quietly. She called these her "sound breaks." Her decision to live in Manhattan, and the settling that comes with time, eventually brought a freedom to blend into the city crunch and chaos by her clock and at her own pace. Somewhere in these last few years, following a move from the Midwest to the East Coast Liz had reclaimed her roots. She described it as "osmosis" as the transformation from "tourist to resident" was so gradual she wasn't aware until one day she was approached for directions and found herself responding quickly and with confidence. Her excursions, although with a destination in mind, were usually peppered with enticing distractions. Displays and posed mannequins in store windows lured her to explore the latest in fashions. And there were her favorite haunts...the street vendors whose array of bargains attracted residents and tourist alike. "Browsing is an art," she would tell herself. These brief departures from the day's agenda added luster and purpose to retirement, however meaningless it may appear to others.

Liz waited for the light at Madison Avenue to change and decided to take the bus up to 50th Street. Once boarded, she quickly found a seat close to the rear door. The ride to St. Patrick's Cathedral was short. It wasn't long before the magnificent carved steeples spiraling over the lesser structures on Fifth Avenue came into view, cutting into the sky, drawing one's gaze heavenly, thus, upward over the tourists and lunch crowd relaxing in a myriad of postures and dress on its stone steps.

Entering the Cathedral, she settled herself into a side pew. Her body tensed against a chill that seemed to come from inside of her. As she aged she noticed the cold didn't wait to react to outside conditions but, instead, rose up unexpectedly inside of her as if triggered by a separate thermometer. She referred to this phenomenon as "inside out." Still, and in spite of seasonal discomforts, she remained staunch against any suggestion of moving to a warmer climate. She nestled deeper into her coat and relaxed into the surrounding warmth. . Soon the silence created a gentle lull. She remembered a recent quote she read, "Seeking silence in the midst of din is like turning yourself over to the angels for a brain massage." She sighed a deep, contented sigh, closed her eyes and relaxed against the back of the pew.

Images floated up from somewhere, definitely dreamlike. She recognized herself sitting on a cushioned chair...at a salon and, instead of a beautician, the mirror in front of her reflected an angel smiling down from behind Liz's chair. Soon Liz felt herself being touched ever so lightly gently, comforting, then rising beneath her as if she were lying on wave swells. Soothing murmurs filling her and carrying her like a feather in a spring breeze. She heard the echo, distant but mysteriously resonating from herself. "There is a whole world living inside of me. Like silent film waiting for sound. I am the narrator and, so, if I place old tapes into rewind and follow up by starting the replay. Of course! There I am! It's me! I am on the big screen! I'm the main character! And yet, it's like I'm viewing it for the first time... in color!" Liz sighed and let herself be carried away.

The year was 1995...a year that often came to mind. It was the year that Jeremy's phone call opened up unimagined events in Liz's life. December and Christmas were due in a month. Liz glanced out the window at the lawn covered in fresh snow and decided that perhaps, this year, Minnesota would have a white Christmas. They had been sparse in recent years.

When the phone rang the noise startled her. "It is too early in the morning for company," she groaned. She treasured those first moments of quiet in the mornings. Any interruptions before seven A.M. and two cups of coffee made her flinch with distress. The intruder must have heard her sigh.

"Hey sister, how would you like to spend Christmas in New York?"

"Hey back to you," she muffled through morning gauze. It was Jeremy! Her mood lifted as his question awakened immediate interest.

"New York? New York! You haven't been in New York for years. In fact," she continued as the direction of their conversation became clearer. "I thought you had turned tropical after living half your life in Florida."

Ignoring her inquiry, he quipped, "So, what do you think about spending Christmas in New York?" If this was an attempt to refocus her, it worked.

"If I say yes, would you clarify? And, please, tell me this does not concern a woman."

"Well, yes and no," he added. They're friends I met in England. He is an interpreter at the U.N. and his wife works on the Dave Letterman Show. I know I'm boring you."

"And for this you interrupted my morning quiet? Her words rippled through laughter. "You're kidding, right? Or this is a dream, huh? Give me fifteen minutes. Let me hit myself in the head a few times and I'll call you back."

Promise?

What do you think?

When they were growing up her brother thrived on attention, but never in a mean or obstinate way. And as he matured so he developed what she described as "finesse." His approach subtle and softened with humor, as if he sensed his role from an early age was to relieve tensions by interjecting his perspective. His humorist skills lightened reality and made even times of adversity bearable. He made us pause. He made us laugh. "Our parents must have sensed it, too. Why else would they have chosen to baptize him "Jeremy Gerard"? Growing up he hated that name." But, she concluded, "life does seem to affirm truth if we live long enough." In his fifties Jeremy was invited to join a local theatre group, at which time he began writing his name "J. Gerard" as if its acceptance affirmed to him and to the world the truth of his destiny. Liz wasn't surprised when years later she learned that, when five years old, Jeremy attended dance class. At dinner one night she became inquisitive to know why he suddenly dropped out after only a few sessions. "Why didn't you stay?" He looked away, smiled pensively, turned his gaze back to her with a look that said, "I've never told anyone." She waited while he sipped his beer, adding to the moment of grand disclosure. And then, when he was ready, he answered, "The damn teacher kept kissing me."

So, that's when it started...women problems...even in kindergarten! Woman of all ages, from adoring nieces to waitresses at the restaurants. Liz began to observe him as he ingratiated himself and brought casual conversation. What was incongruous was that the waitress never seemed noticeably impatient with this tall, Docker-clad, ageless man's demands for an extra dinner napkin, for instance, onto which he neatly lined his silverware like a surgeon strategically placing his instruments, If they thought his request for "just a half a cup of coffee" was eccentric enough, especially when he proceeded to pour the overfill into his sister's cup if she went over "half," they never showed it. By the time he got to "the sauce on the side and no butter on the toast," Liz was convinced she was the only sane one of the three of them. This routine repeated itself so often Liz became resigned. "It must be me," she would tell herself. Because, by the time they made their exit, the woman whom Liz had just observed pleasantly complying with her brother's meticulous demands, acted like she had been graced.

"And maybe, just maybe she was," Liz reevaluated. Perhaps once in a great while a man arrives for dinner whose presence and interest shown to her is refreshing, and if she happens to be at the end of her shift, takes her mind off her aching feet. "Who can figure?" And, then one day a little cell in Liz's head popped. "And I bet that rascal brother of mine gives big tips, too!"

Ten minutes later she dialed him. He answered,

"You're early. You couldn't give me that last five minutes to reconsider my offer?"

"It's dangerous to commit before you're feet are on the floor Now that I'm awake, will you fill in the part that was interrupted by my hanging up on you."

"I accept your apology. Soooo, I am mailing you a ticket, round trip, all paid for, and have already arranged for us to stay at the Y in Manhattan."

"My sugar daddy brother, am I hearing you say you are treating me to another great adventure. And I use that word, 'adventure,' because I am still suffering from flashbacks of our last trip together.

"Wounds heal. So... I 'm waiting."

"Yes!"

"You won't be sorry."

"Yes, I will. But I'm grateful, so excitedly grateful!"

"Yes," he answered, feigning exhaustion.

"You are a sweetheart and I love you."

"Yes, I know."

Liz's attention immediately went to the clock on her bed stand. She grabbed her robe from the foot of her bed and bolted for the shower. Her new shower head sprayed down with pin point touches of pleasure. "Hmm," she moaned and tilted her head into the spray. She was surprised by how quickly the fine needles of pleasure transported her back to luxuries she and Jeremy had enjoyed at the hotel in Charlotte this past summer. She followed the images back, back, until her memory rested on this white-steepled building set back from the road in a cluster of trees. They were late for the wedding. Jeremy had insisted they stop for coffee and a muffin. Never mind the fact that they left Charlotte knowing this was unfamiliar territory and their arrival could be hampered by directional dysfunction.

All of which materialized as they found themselves driving around aimlessly, Jeremy, looking confident after his recent intake of sugar, was relaxed. However, Liz, realizing she was going to see their relatives for the first time in years, began to panic. Her eyes grew wild and she noticed with embarrassment she began to pant as her head jerked from side to side and up and down checking the map. If they had been stopped by police at that moment, she was positive the officer would notice the silent scream in her expression and decide that she was being held hostage. Worse still, if he then surmised that the driver, who by now was showing signs of agitation, was clearly hiding a gun in the blazer lying on the seat between them. That is when, it seemed, divine intervention took over. Jeremy noticed the white steeple through the ridge of trees above them.

As they entered into what they hurriedly calculated was the lobby, since it was immediately situated inside the front doors, Liz jolted to a stop and braced leaving Jeremy to run into her from behind. Standing directly in front of them stood the bride and her father. Simultaneously expression and color drained from the father's face. The bride's arm shot up with opened hand as if someone flipped a switch for an oncoming train. Liz hurled herself into a corner leaving Jeremy standing glued to his spot. He just stood there! For a moment his face wore a familiar studied look that she knew meant, "What the ...?" Only this time, Liz recalled, Jeremy looked like the curtain went up before he had read the script. Realizing his conscious thought was leading him nowhere, she seized the situation. Quickly she surmised, "The wedding party, maid of honor, bridesmaids and even the ushers were nowhere in sight. The wedding has already started!"

Recovering from her rapid summation and its implications, she noticed the bride and her father had pulled back from the center aisle and were gesturing frantically to Jeremy, who had just replaced them in the doorway. Everyone's attention was riveted in gushing expectation on the flowered arch which only a few seconds before had framed the bride in flowing silk and lace. Instead, paused motionless in this space of sacred ritual, stood a slender figure with white hair in a borrowed blazer and a 1970's J. C. Penney shirt and tie. Liz, drowning now in a wave of terror when she realized what was happening, gasped. And on the exhale, managed to whisper, "Jeremy, come here." Like a muted scream she repeated his name. "Jeremy! Move!" He spun around and, like the family pet called from the path of a semi, he came towards her, "almost as if," she recalled, "by learned command."

They stood there in the corner together, hearing the organist, obviously recovered, begin the bridal march. And, like two people who had crossed a line and narrowly escaped a border patrol, they gazed into space. Liz was numb. She had left Jeremy standing in the center of the doorway where everyone's eyes were focused expecting to see the bride. She had jumped into the last life boat and left her brother to drown! Her guilt was short-lived. Later, feeling the healing effects of numerous champagne toasts, a member of the bridal party introduced himself. He enjoyed relating what he heard from his close proximity to the altar. The minister had leaned over to the groom and asked, "Who is that?" To which the groom, never having met Jeremy, adjusted his gaze for a second look and answered, "Darned if I know."

Liz turned off the shower and was transported back to the present. But not before the images emerged of their nieces and nephews standing in the front rows of this small church trying to contain themselves. Each one was obviously racked in personal contortions. Some just gave in and muffled their hysterics with their hands. The parents of the bride, planned and, she was sure, paid the price for this "perfect wedding" for their only daughter. The groom's military guard provided pomp and pageantry. Relatives from all over the east coast were invited, as well as friends, and people of position and rank in the community. "And who became the topic of conversation later when everyone gathered at the Country Club? You betcha. That man in the doorway." Jeremy had done it again. Only this time whether premeditated or unconsciously it didn't matter to Liz. Her brother's minor part gained him more attention than the bride and groom on their wedding day. To Liz this was unforgiveable. . However, with time she became confused, that is, after repeatedly witnessing the tremors in the room from laughter as The "Wedding Story" was retold at family gatherings. After pondering the paradox she decided it was all about control. "It's almost like in the face of stressful formality, Jeremy's eccentricities catch people off guard. The retelling of events must tickle with just enough whimsy to affirm the potential for human comedy present in every desperate attempt at perfection. Writers make big money creating situations that seem to play out so naturally in Jeremy's world."

Dressed and searching the cupboard for cereal, Liz began singing, "New York, New York, what a wonderful town," but stopped abruptly. "I'm going to New York with Jeremy. God help us!"

> Winter moods,
> dark and grey day.
> Snow dusted, ice crusted images
> fueling our dismay.

Words taken from my mother's journal. Unfortunately it was the year I was born!" It was years later that Liz would come to understand the grief that fueled those few lines. "We won't go there," she whispered under her frosted breath. Her thoughts kept time with the crunch of her boots on the ice as she made her way through the parking lot. She had begun the morning with an excitement brought on by her brother's phone call. However, insipidly, like toxic vapor, the week's "uglies" began to seep in unnoticed. That is, until a sudden irritability gripped her as she pulled in late for Tuesday's board meeting. She drew in a deep breath and exhaled slowly as the car engine died. Her fleeting attempts at breath control worked. As she quickened her steps the source of her growing unrest became clearer. This vexed turnaround was triggered, she recalled, when she stepped into zero weather and realized she had forgotten to put her car into the garage the night before. As predicted, "and why this time the weather people had to be accurate!" she calculated two inches of snow lay on the driveway and mounded gracefully over the contours of her car. "When am I going to take the forecasts seriously and retrieve my scraper from the trunk." Her beloved little Cooper groaned from under its hood as if traumatized by her neglect. Frustration was added when, arriving at the office, she realized she hadn't added closure to the proposal she planned to present to the Board. She would have to wing it. Hurriedly entering her office, and ignoring the light flashing on her phone she gathered the papers she had left scattered on her desk the night before and walked toward the staff room.

It had been two years since taking on the position in pastoral care at the parish. The first year had brought anticipation of change and a fresh start. St. Joseph's was a small urban parish. Growing up in New York during the 50's had prepared her adequately for her ministry to the predominantly Irish-Italian post-war population. By her second year at the little urban church, the neighborhood was showing notable signs of change, Because of the size and 50's charm of its houses, young singles and couples looking for starter homes began moving into the postwar tangle of dwellings circling the little church. In addition, an influx of Hmong and Hispanics to Minnesota drew a large immigrant population to the urban center, resulting in noticeable cultural changes in neighborhoods close to their small eastside community. It soon became clear to Liz that the face of this area for the second half of the century was already in flux for area churches and community centers. To her it appeared obvious events were not waiting for her parishioners to adapt at a moderate pace. On the contrary, like everything else in the late 20th century, these changes were overwhelming to those who had lived simply and unchanged for years, as had the parishioners of St. Joseph's. Liz took her place at the board table and perused the room. Most likely, by need, her attention was drawn to the first friendly face.

Anne, the Youth Formation Director, was pouring coffee. Needing a few extra moments to collect herself, Liz slid a cup off the shelf and joined her. "Good morning." Her voice sounded strange and frozen. Anne gave a full smile, communicating she may have chosen not to notice. "Hi! Did you have to dig your way out this morning?" she asked pleasantly. "Oh, I forgot. You're one of those lucky urban dwellers who has a garage."

Anne's playful attempt at envy confused Liz. She looked up from her cup. "Convenience works if you remember to use it," she mustered. "I forgot and left my car out last night. This morning was not a pretty sight!" Perhaps it was the tone of Anne's voice...modulated... but still pitched "to land over the plate." A learned skill. Opera singers claim the trained voice has the capability of reaching the furthest seats in the balcony using breath control. She was brought back to attention by Anne's remark as she nodded towards Liz. "So that explains your death grip on that cup," to which she added, "Cream?" Liz met her inquiry with a forced "Thank you," hoping it eased the tight crisp tones of her initial morning stance.

In more pensive moments Liz wondered about Anne's balanced presence on staff. While Liz worked at restraining her reactions, Anne's ability to keep focused under stress was enviable. "Cool" is the word Liz used to describe Anne. Sometimes she caught innuendos that left her wondering if Anne's reticence at meetings was a cover for tensions similar to her own. Then there were her moments of rationalization during which Liz convinced herself that Anne felt more comfortable and safe with the status quo of the staff. Naturally, this would allow her to operate free of the inquisitions imposed upon Liz, her rattled associate. "My being the new member was bound to cause a few ripples on the waters of years of a traditional and repetitive system. Shame on you, Lizzie girl, for such small thinking." While she was leery of encouraging thoughts that flirted on the edge of paranoia, at the same time, "peace at any cost" was not Liz's mode of operation. As a result, she often found herself at odds with certain members of staff whose resistance to her was a constant irritant. Some days she lamented, "It's difficult to distinguish which of us is feeling more threatened by the other!"

As agenda dictated, the next two hours were focused on the various ministries which appeared on the agenda...sacramental, liturgical, youth, hospitality and, Liz would repeat to herself, "finances, finances and finances." For the past two years her attempts to form an outreach to new neighbors, as well as a plan for an adult formation program remained low on the list of priorities. Still, she had been able to establish a library. In addition, the success of Cana Night for couples pleased her. This morning, however, she was not prepared, and this morning she was, as she described afterwards, "in a dangerous mood." Needless to explain any further, before conceding to adjournment, and working without notes, Liz decided to go down extemporaneously. What could she lose? Past resistance had already convinced her that she was a pest, a virus, a low-grade infectious tick, sent to weaken their perfectly coordinated operation. She looked around to bolster her confidence. She noticed Anne leaning back against her chair as if already planning her escape. Father Kemp's shoulders sagged suspecting, she was certain, that his good nature was about to be tested. Then, regaining his familiar pastoral composure, he reached for a donut and settled back in his chair.

Liz glanced over at Nancy, pen paused, looking nervously around the room but, nevertheless, as always, her faithful diligence to her position as receptionist and administrative assistance drew her focus back to the minutes. Liz waited and then began, "I will speak slowly so that you may write down every word. If not for its impact in the present...at least for posterity when they open our time capsule. The Church," and she emphasized, "with a capital C, seems to have no problem ministering to the newborn, very young, and to the dying. However, it is the mature adult, yes, those among the living, who are drifting in the gap between the two. These are my concern...and may I remind you of my job description...which clearly names a 'Social Concerns' as well as a 'Social Justice' outreach. Thus, noting these are expectations for adult mission, wouldn't you say? Years and many meetings with church staffs about the subject of Adult Ministry has produced a shared frustration with those who are given the responsibility of an adult outreach and, yet, who exhaust ourselves with programs, we report, do not work! What saddens me and also, may I add, accompanies the responsibility of my pastoral position, is the insistence here at St. Joseph's that we do not need to pursue a response to the adults in our own parish. Why not? This is...we are church...Christ's body. That means we are a living organism, creating, being recreated, growing, stretching, listening...listening!" Are we listening to the times?

Liz's last words ended abruptly as she fought to inhale enough air to finish what she had started. "Love is ongoing. God didn't create us and say, "It is finished"...God said, "It is good." "Good" leaves a lot to the imagination. Revelation is God fulfilling his original plan. It didn't stop with Jesus as if we have it all figured out, or at the Council of Trent or the printing of the Baltimore Catechism or Vatican Two Council! These were just guides on a long journey. Love is work! As church we emphasize the dignity of every human being, "from birth to end of life." Quote, unquote. Birth to death. What I am trying to understand," and her voice grew stronger, "and what I am asking is, what are we doing to, fill the space in between?"

"What I am proposing," she continued after drawing a breath and noticing Anne leaning forward, her gaze fixed on Liz and the good padre holding onto his donut midway to his mouth, "is a fresh approach to ministering to the adults It's not only common sense but becoming imperative that we begin to address the needs of adults, parents, singles, and may I emphasize again, those who have moved into the houses down the street. These ordinary people who have to deal with overwhelming issues of contemporary society and are looking for someone to make sense out of their lives. We can't leave it up to therapists. If God doesn't work in our realities what good is God!"

Her outburst transmitted to her hands which, she realized were gesturing forcefully, propelled by some dynamic energy. "This is a serious world. And we, the church, have to get serious. If we aren't serving the whole Body, and just acting out of small minds, that is, what is convenient for us, then what good are we? A quote I recently heard clarifies my presentation today, 'How long are we going to continue to educate the children and play with the adults?'" Silence followed. As she gathered her papers, she felt light- headed, as if the top of her head had opened and was letting in a delightful breeze. Without looking back, Liz floated out of the room.

She continued taking one step, another step, until she reached the confines of her office. Pushing the door closed behind her, she sunk into her chair and released her hold on the papers in her arms. After an endless space of time with her head resting on her folded arm, Liz raised herself and blinked. The brown bag with her lunch remained where she had tossed it when she arrived. She was grateful for the quiet where she settled in with her hastily made peanut butter sandwich and the cup of cold leftover coffee before returning to the afternoon's phone messages.

Jeremy's phone call has set her whole day behind, including her dinner with Jen. Her friend was early, as usual. Or was Liz consistently late? No matter. Jen's smile and look of expectation as she entered absolved her. Her friend rose and opened her arms when she saw Liz. Jen's warm welcome eased Liz's mood. She met Jen's smile with her own and walked into her embrace. "Sorry I'm late," she mumbled from Jen's neck through a mass of tangled red hair.

"Do I look surprised?" Jen asked.

Liz stepped back and her eyes surveyed her friend's face. She faked annoyance. "Couldn't you try being surprised sometimes? Just to make me feel better."

Jen was not just a person, "Jen is an experience," Liz used to explain to people. "Once you meet her, you never forget her."

That said, Jen's voice interrupted Liz's thoughts. "Sit down and stop your whining." With their familiar roles established, they relaxed and pulled their chairs up to the table to settled in.

That's when Jen leaned over to Liz, her eyes boring into Liz's. "You're having a bad day."

She could always command Liz to full attention with that "look." "Oh, no!" Liz exclaimed, "is it that noticeable?"

Her friend gave that knowing smile. It was the intensity of her eyes that burned their way into Liz's and continued until the heat seared a path through to her brain. Liz referred to it as "Jen's prosecutor's stare." It prepared Liz for either a concerned nudge for information or, in some cases, a direct interrogation. Jen had a skill for sensing secrets, especially when she suspected the secret concerned her. For that matter, anything hidden seemed to stir up the sleuth within her. They had laughed when Jen gave a full account of her devious methods for tracking hiding places and peeking into her presents before Christmas. That inquisitive and crafty little girl was alive and active in Jen, the woman. It was this woman who was paused across the table from her now, waiting, waiting for Liz to reveal what keen perception had sensed from their first moments of greeting. Jen was scary.

Liz, attempting to shade herself from the blaze of the inquisitor, looked directly into Jen's eyes, she blurted, "You're scary."

"And you're evasive. Do you know how maddening that is?"

"No. I don't. I'm a Cancer. Cancers are supposed to be evasive. We're water signs. We flow."

"And what, may I ask, is flowing behind that dark, confused look?"

"Ambivalence."

"Ambivalence? Oh, that's a good word!"

"I think it means your mental processes are ambling, or hovering, between ignorance and absolute conclusion." Liz attempted to explain. Jen's face tensed and her lip got tight.

"Now I'm the one feeling ambivalent. How about we get back to a word I understand, like 'flow.' I can work with that. And speaking of 'flow,' as in 'liquid,'" she added, "shall we have a drink before dinner?"

"You betcha,'" Liz fired back, relieved.

Jen's face relaxed. "Don't we have fun?"

Manhattans and onion rings. These always preceded the main course as a ritual of sisterhood. Liz couldn't remember how it started. It may have been when Jen was going through a divorce. Or maybe when Liz had gotten laid off and was trying to survive the recession of the 80's. Whatever it was and however it began, it worked. Before the evening ended each parted with, if not solutions, definitely fresh perspective on life's issues, in addition to the free sharing that softened the cutting edges. And, of course, there was the laughter that always preceded the parting and set the course for a lighter response to whatever lay ahead... until their next meeting.

Relaxed and sipping their drinks, Jen dipped into the catsup, popped an onion ring into her mouth. "Can you believe how long it's been since we discovered the therapeutic value of a Manhattan with a plate of fried onion rings?"

Liz pretended to shudder. "Don't bring it up. If I remember I may have a cholesterol attack right here in front of you. I'd go to the hospital and you would have to pay for dinner."

Jen countered, "Oh, no,...I'd make the ambulance wait until you finished explaining 'ambivalent.'"

Hearing her cue for expose' Liz shared, "The positive is that I am going to New York."

"Exciting! When?"

"Over Christmas. Actually I began the day on that high note."

"Your day began on a high note? And only hours later you come dragging into dinner! Who died between then and now?"

Liz dipped and onion ring and ignored Jen's sarcasm. "Are you going to let me finish? It began with Jeremy's phone call."

"Jeremy? You are going to New York with your brother Jeremy! The brother who pays for everything and takes you on these exciting trips. Oh, yes," she continued, "I can see now why you're depressed. Having someone offer an all-expense-paid trip to New York is enough to make a person suicidal."

Jen could deliver clipped wit with such a straight face that, if you didn't catch it immediately, you would miss the humor. Liz had learned to catch it in flight, and hold onto it while it jarred her out of self-pity.

"If you think that's ridiculous, wait until I tell you about my grand presentation at the church." The account made Liz breathless and she paused. "Drats! The euphoria of victory faded by the time I reached my office And, if that isn't wimpy enough, I hid in my office all afternoon. How does that sound, speaking of ambivalence. When it came time for my presentation something happened. I was fierce, I was eloquent, I was woman! I left them stunned...or..," she reconsidered, "just maybe I was the one stunned."

They were still silent as I walked from the room. Liz felt herself light and breathless again as she explained her stand before the Board. "But then," she said, and her eyes dulled and she reached for her drink, "after I went back to my office and closed the door I panicked."

What did I do? What did I say? I'm not really sure, except it felt like someone else took over and for those few minutes it felt like I was listening to someone outside of myself. And I was cheering her on. It was as if I were two of me.

Jen's expression softened and she reached across for Liz's hand, "Honey, you were being You... both of You. You were being Liz...God's Liz speaking out for all those you know need a voice. It's like the Liz who likes to please and the gutsy warrior Liz were in sync. Liz climbed on her horse and yelled 'Charge!' It's powerful when that happens. Don't you understand yet? All these years you have ministered to people, listening to them. teaching, writing programs, sharing what is real from your own journey instead of what you learned from a book. Now you are saying things that need to be said. And some people get upset. So what! Did you expect to be treated better than Jesus was?" She lifted her glass, "Here's to you, Liz McKenna, may you never again be afraid to be yourself and to speak the truth."

Liz reached for her glass, and as she did, she realized what a treasure she found in Jen's friendship, which, of course prompted her to attempt another toast. Moved and grateful, she could only whisper, "Thank you."

"During the meal, Jen asked, "Have I said this before? If you would join the Episcopal church you could be ordained." Liz looked up from her meal and grinned. "Only about every other month or two for the last ten years. Now why would I want to be ordained?" she asked.

"Because you could have power." Jen stated.

"You're pretty emphatic about that." Liz grinned between chews. "I guess you're right, Jen But, there again, I've served side by side with priests and we related to one another as equals. Power doesn't give anyone permission to control. When I've found myself in a position of power I discovered the awesome responsibility that comes with it. "To much is given, much is expected", remember? I've known for a long time that I wouldn't make a very good priest. Facing people before eight in the morning I find intolerable, as well as donning those heavy vestments on a hot summer day. And, speaking of vestments, your frame looks better in liturgical robes, You are imposing even out of vestments Your frame and height commands instant interest and respect. Me? I am skinny, a frame that bounces when in rapid motion. For this reason I have to work at being imposing, prove my credibility in the first few moments of my presentation. I draw more attention in a Calvin Klein black suit and white classic shirt. I have to work harder to be taken seriously by persons raised in culture of male authenticity. When I don a vestment I've been accused of grandstanding. My personality is diminished. I get lost in the folds, buried in the bulk...whatever." Liz knew by Jen's stern expression that her presentation was mesmerizing. She continued with a final statement of disclosure. And, and... liturgy with all of its grandeur and solemnity, with its precise rituals, would wear me out to no useful purpose. I am just not graced for that calling. And... and..." she repeated with emphasis, "this may astound you, but being Catholic gives me joy."

Jen raised her eyebrows. "Really. Then why have I spent the last hour and a half lifting you out of the pit?"

Liz grasped for a solid comeback. "Because we are community. That's it! When I'm in the pit, you lower the rope and pull me out. When you're drowning I leap in and lift you up. Sharing the human condition is not for wimps. Whenever I feel defeated and want to flee I remember a comment from a priest and it helps me gain perspective about the Catholic Church, He said, 'Holy Mother, the Church, is like your own mother. You love her. But sometimes she infuriates you. What are you going to do? You can't shoot her.'"

Jen's stifled swallow came out like a snort. And then she started to laugh. To avoid choking, Liz had stopped eating. Jen's sudden reaction triggered a laugh too explosive to contain. Their outburst interrupted a man at the table next to them who looked up, fork still paused on its way to his mouth. His eyes sparkled with amusement. "You girls have to lighten up!"

Jen calmed first. "Goodness...and what is this obsession with mothers? Oops. Don't tell me. You've got the answer."

Liz wiped the last of the tears from her eyes and straightened up for another stab at the profound. "Are you ready for this? The answer is, mothers are the last to give up on you and, sadly, the last to be forgiven by you."

Jen was the first to break the silence that followed. "Do you want to know what I think? I think you should stay off the Manhattans."

Chapter 2

Liz's dinner with Jen had worked its magic. This morning she drove to the church feeling renewed and confident. The quiet as she entered assured her that the staff were engaged in their offices, including Nancy, whose first duties were always returning calls and greeting parishioners who came to the receptionist window after the morning Mass. Nancy's graciousness at all hours of the day, her full body, soft voice and nurturing attentiveness, with which she gave rapt attention to all matters great and trivial, assured everyone of acceptance and, for some, a listening ear for sharing personal concerns.

Today, however, it was obvious that other things occupied Nancy's thoughts as she walked from her office and proceeded down the hall. Liz greeted her as she approached. "Are you busy"? Liz knew that furtive look. Nancy's duties gave her privy to a mass of information. Thus, her quickened steps and whispered tones prepared Liz for the prelude to something brewing that could be serious enough to warrant secrecy.

"Okay," was Liz's greeting. "What's going on?" Since the staff meeting she tried to hold off the anticipated confrontation. She sighed with resignation observing Nancy searching the hall area for some possible persons within earshot.

"I tried to call you last night, but you were out."

"Why didn't you leave me a message?" Liz countered.

"I don't know...I guess it was rather late. That clarified, she began,

"After you left yesterday there wasn't much said. Anne can give you some of our conversation later. I just want you to warn you that Fr, Kemp will want to see you when he returns from hospital calls.

"Well, that doesn't surprise me, considering I threw firecrackers into the fire pit yesterday and ran before they went off. That was spineless behavior on my part."

Nancy waited for her to complete the last sentence, before continuing. The phone rang. She bolted to the desk and responded mechanically into the receiver, "St. Joseph's Church. May I help you?" Her conversation blurred into the backdrop of Liz's rapid thoughts as she felt her cheeks becoming hot. She turned her focus to the garden outside to divert the growing panic, while repeating to herself, "Calm down...that's it...calm down...just...and then when tactics failed to calm her. If whoever is on the other end of that phone doesn't get off soon I am going to lunge at Nancy and jerk the phone out of her tight little hand!"

She turned when she heard the click and stared wildly into Nancy's questioning gaze. "Like I should have held my breath waiting for your message! I'd be unconscious by now! What?" she projected as quietly as she was able to subdue exasperation. Noticing Nancy's retreat Liz paused so perhaps both of them could restart from their initial greetings earlier. Calmed now, Liz's panic eased and she was able to direct her inquiry in a softer tone. "What is it you are trying to tell me?"

Nancy, recouped and encouraged by Liz's change of tone, began. "A woman came into church yesterday afternoon. She had a young girl with her. They were Hmong. The woman was so agitated she jerked all over. In between sentences she was crying and dabbing her eyes. When Father came out to greet them, the girl, whom we learned was her daughter, Mai Lee , told him that their mother was very upset. Then she explained that it was because her six year old brother refused to attend school today. When she questioned him, he told her, "It's those people in the big building, I'm afraid."

Liz's face must have shown the confusion she felt. Mary paused while Liz felt behind her for her chair and Nancy settled into the other.

"Did you have children here for the Thanksgiving food drive last week?"

"Well, yes. We did an outreach to the children in the neighborhood school. They came in classes, about four groups, and brought staples and can goods for the Thanksgiving Baskets." Liz replayed the event in her mind. "Remember? I came to your office later and shared what a precious experience it was. Little children parading in. Excited, inquisitive, asking so many questions."

"Do you remember a little boy stopping at the foot of the crucifix?"

"Yes. A little Hmong child. He was so small he had to bend his head way back to focus He became transfixed...awestruck as I remember now."

The two women were so concentrated neither noticed the figure who had taken up position in the doorway. Nancy jumped. "Excuse me, I have to get back to my desk." Fr. Kemp stepped aside to let her pass, after which he entered and sat down. "Please," he encouraged, "continue."

Liz exhaled to focus her thoughts back to the boy standing below the crucifix. "He stood there for the longest time," she continued, "and then he asked, 'Who is that?' I answered, 'Jesus.' He became very quiet. Without taking his eyes off Jesus he asked me, 'What happen'?' in this cute accent."

At this point in her telling, her eyes squinted with tension as she tried to recall the exact words of the encounter.

Father Kemp coached her, "What did you tell him?"

"That they killed Jesus." With this Liz threw her hands up and said, "Oh, no! I didn't say 'they.' Oh, God! Instead (.and why, I don't know) I said 'we.' WE killed Jesus!"

The priest sat back in his chair and nodded. "Well, that's good theology, Liz, but hardly conducive to encouraging a little child's faith. At least I know now what led up to the Hmong woman's visit."

Liz, remorseful, defenses down, addressed him by his first name. "Paul...I am so sorry. I never gave a thought to how it would be interpreted by him! What can I do or say to undue this mess? Without meaning to, my use of words traumatized this poor child. " The priest's expression validated her last statement.

"With her daughter, Mai Lee, as interpreter, the mother said that her son did not want to go back to school because the people in the building down the block kill people and hang them up on the wall." Liz groaned imagining a meat cooler and began massaging her pounding temples."

"Why didn't I take the time and think before I answered." She drew in a deep breath and let it out slowly. She forced her gaze to meet his. "What do I do? How do I fix it?"

He waited as if to leave time for any further comment from her and then answered, "You've done enough, don't you think? And you can thank me for being around at the right time". His tone softened. "And, yes, as you discovered, sharing the profound calls us to pause to ponder the questions. Even greater is our response to the awe and curiosity of a child. It demands that we stop our busyness and think before we speak. I suspect we all, as I do, forget the deep wisdom that is expressed in a child's observations. My years in ministry have taught me a few things." Then his eyes lit with amusement and he added, "That's why they call me 'Boss.'"

This said, he moved towards the door and glanced back. "I am going to grab a cup of coffee and I'll be in my office. If there are no urgent distractions, we will continue our conversation there."

Liz was motionless and unblinking as her eyes followed his tall figure retreating down the hall. Then it dawned soft and reassuring. Through this perplexing situation she was learning a side of her priest she never realized until this morning.

True to his suggestion, and after both were seated, Fr. Paul returned them to the subject at hand. "And, so, I'll tell you what I did. Naturally, I invited our guests to sit in chapel with me. They waited and I zipped into Anne's office and explained my dilemma. She gave me a child's book on 'The Life of Jesus,' which I gave to them and told them they could keep. I explained as briefly as I could, knowing the need to keep it simple. "Jesus, I explained, was the most loving and perfect human being that ever lived. Mai Lee relayed my words to her mother. In the second it took for this tiny women's understanding to click in, she fired off a question to her daughter. Mai Lee turned to me and asked in her mother's words, "Then why did you kill him?"

Liz drew in her breath. The priest took a sip from his cup and then continued. "This is what I have uncovered after all my years gathering wisdom to support the answers. The scrutiny of the simple cuts deep. Still, I have to say, this woman's question startled me, but it also clarified something to me. And it was a rising awareness of her journey, her sacrifices, and the plight of her people in Laos. Perhaps, it was in that clarity I suddenly concluded, it was possible to explain to someone like her why the people Jesus came to save turned on him. Or maybe, as I think now, she had already begun to understand. Those in power that she trusted, and some she loved like her own, she shared with me through her tears, turned on her and her family, her people, and betrayed them and killed them. When I asked her how she survived and was still teaching her children to believe in their future. "Where does your hope come from?" I asked. She spoke three words I didn't understand. Her daughter repeated to me in English, "I chose love."

He took a breath and then continued. "It was then that I knew how to answer her question and calm her little boy's fears at the same time. I told her that when her son reads about Jesus he will also look at the pictures. Pictures of Jesus holding a lamb, laughing with children, visiting friends, teaching in the religious temple.

Paul pushed his seat back and spread his arms out. He shot the question across and over the desk. "Why don't we have one of these pictures hung on the main wall over our altar?" His quickness of movement catapulted the question with thrust directly at her enough to slice the air and bring Liz to full attention. He repeated it with emphasis, "Why don't we have one of those pretty pictures hanging over the altars?" Liz, alerted by his passion, like a jet breaking the sound barrier, managed to bleat, "Why?"

"Why indeed. Why, instead, do we have this man hanging on a cross, stripped and bleeding out?" The priest rolled back into his desk and looked at Liz's rapt expression "The answer came to me as instantly as the question! It illuminated for me a truth that I repeated to myself committing it to memory before I lost it in the sharing. And, so, I took my time. I began slowly, "The reason we were led to choose the cross as a centerpoint of our faith is," and I watched Mai Lee and her mother move closer as I continued, "is precisely because, in its stark and horrifying truth, it convicts, and it asks the same question as you just asked of me, "Why did we kill him? "

Evidently satisfied he made his point, he stood up. He took a deep breath and allowed his gaze to settle on the crucifix that hung on the wall behind her. Seemingly, drawing on grace, he sat down again and continued. "There are times when explaining our faith to someone so eager to listen sparks our own renewal."

"We...yes, we...us... All of us... we Christians carry the burden of Jesus' death. To justify, to blame, to forget makes us vulnerable to a repeat of our actions. Instead, thank God, we continue to live gratefully in the shadow of that cross, while, as Christians, our faith keeps us in the hope in what awaits us on the other side of it."

By this time Liz wondered if her face carried the frown that she was sure reflected the strain of forced retention.

"And, no!" her priest blurted suddenly before showing signs of wearing down. I didn't get into the resurrection. Poor Mai Lee would have had quite a struggle relaying that part of the story. At this final conjecture, Liz was silently sympathizing with Mai Lee's plight.

"No...my sense told me, God willing, that dear little woman may be inspired to return to hear the sequel. I chose my words carefully. "Every day,' I told her, "like you, we who follow Jesus choose love. And when we are tempted otherwise, to lash out, to stray or become weary, that cross remains before us as a reminder of what we are capable of when we give in to the fear that propels us to do violence."

"Ahh," and the mother nodded as if she understood. And even before Mai Lee, bless her, struggled to repeat my words to her. It was a good sound...reassuring. We shared just enough. Sensing this, I made a motion towards the door, but not before I invited her and her family to our Christmas pageant." Liz looked lost as if struggling with reentry to the moment "So," as he revived again, "how did I do?" he asked.

"Wow!' she exclaimed, like one walking out of the theatre grasping for a return to reality. "You done good. Wow! Who is this marvel who leaps over tall obstacles?" But, her mood quickly reverted to the initial effect of the trauma she caused. "Ugh! I really feel terrible!" She waited before sharing. "You know, before I came here it seemed my ministering was consistently blessed. Everything I did seemed to bear fruit. Maybe it was naiveté, or I'm expecting too much too soon, or perhaps suffering from grand illusions. Whatever. It seems since I arrived at the parish so much of what I try to accomplish falls flat...like ventures into futility. Frustration builds until, like yesterday, I combust all over the Board and then...this! I seem to accomplish little and aggravate much. She drew her gaze from space to look at him "...so pleased, so confident...so priestly in his plaid shirt" she noted to herself.

"Really?" he responded as he rose and walked with her to the door. He turned to her. "Fruitless, huh? Futile? Aggravating? Are you so sure of that?"

With a smile and, as Liz later related to Anne, "he was beamed up from the doorway". Her humor conveyed the new dimension impressed upon her of a man whom, just a day before, she thought she knew. She shared her confusion.

She did it again! Poised and calm, Anne sat listening.

"Maybe, after some time you will want to share your fresh perspective with Father Paul."

Liz studied her associate and let her thoughts follow Anne's suggestion.

"How do you do that?"

"How do I do what?" Anne's eyes sparked with interest.

"How do you take my emotionally charged, thousand-word recitation of the last ten minutes and summarize with a brief sentence? And have it make sense? How did you become so sensible?"

Anne's response was familiar. She accepted compliments with the drop of her eyes, and with a modest smile as her cheeks flushed.

"I guess, if what you're saying about me is true, it came from growing up on a farm. Spontaneity took a back seat to the natural laws of survival. Growing up in a farm family taught me to respect the positives from team effort. Anne became more thoughtful..."Now that you've asked, I'm reflecting and have to say, living so close to all the things in life that could thwart our best efforts, like storms, draughts, the markets, ...things beyond our control, makes me less reactive to things that seem smaller in comparison. I'm sappy enough to think all these things we let drag us down will play out in time...

Liz was startled as Anne began chuckling like someone opening a box and discovering her baby pictures. She turned to Liz. "Thanks. You've made me realize a gift I overlooked. I can see I turn out my best efforts working in a team."

They remained seated in a reflective quiet. Fortified by a fresh respect for Anne's disclosures, Liz chose honesty. Deciding to follow the modest approach, she responded with a humility that surprised herself. "Maybe this big city girl needs an angel of common sense to add some balance." Finding herself in strange territory, without her usual blustery confidence to guide her, Liz was relieved when her attention was drawn to the clock on the wall. "Oops, it's getting late. So, oh, Wise One, have you any parting words with which to bless me?"

"Hey! We're missing coffee break!" With this, Anne rose to leave and then turned to face Liz.

"You're really hard on men, you know."

> Feet, feet,
> all kinds of feet,
> in heavy shoes,
> boots cropped,
> high topped,
> leather bound,
> rubber round...

...and then there was the one pair of feet wearing white tennis shoes...in December!

And with thermometers reading twenty-four degrees at last check! These were the feet that drew Liz's focus while she simultaneously bent into the wind. Flakes of fine snow pelted her cheeks and stung her eyes as she tried desperately to concentrate on that one pair of feet in rapid motion directly in front of her. The intensity of her efforts was eased a bit by the stark contrast of white tennis shoes against the brigade of winter footwear as New Yorkers rushed through their lunch breaks. Her concentration was suddenly interrupted when Jeremy's hand reached back and began to pull her from the crowd towards a revolving door. Inside, her eyes blinked out of the wet blur and onto letters spelling out S A K S. They were in Saks, Saks Fifth Avenue! Whatever her discomfort was a moment before, it all dissolved as her eyes followed the sparkle of silvery gauze dancing above them with a graceful flow of ribbons and lights. The atmosphere was draped in pearl and silver tones and, a piano played softly in the distance. The clanging, the bell ringing, the wind and the din of the street closed off with the lap of the revolving door sounding behind them.

"Wow!" Liz heard the excitement in her voice and added, "I sound like a kid on her first Christmas morning. Wow, this is beautiful!" She turned around and realized Jeremy was not beside her. Gazing around, she spotted him sitting on a bench by the entrance. He wore a cap of snow on the top of his head and, as he bent to remove the snow from the insides of his shoes, a cascade of cold crystals ran down his cheek. Liz felt into her purse for Kleenex. "I suppose it never dawned on you to bring some winter gear." "Didn't have time," he mumbled mopping the cold drops from his cheek. That's when she noticed people pausing in the entrance as they freed themselves from the revolving door into the light. She observed their interest as they removed scarfs, hats and gloves and pondered her brother. Their expressions and obvious scrutiny seemed to ask, "Why is that nut wearing white tennis shoes?" New Yorkers aren't coy. "There are a million stories in the big city," she repeated to herself. Along with subway stories she decided Jeremy, if he continued visiting, would provide his share.

A mixture of gratitude and child-like expectation kept bubbling up as the day unfolded.

In spite of pretenses of resisting Jeremy's initial invitation, her need to claim some space from ministry became more evident as the weeks passed. This, added to the loneliness she had begun to feel during the holidays, intensified her urgency to act on her brother's offer. A week after Thanksgiving her plane ticket to New York had arrived.

She stood at the mailbox staring at the unopened envelope. "Lordy, Lordy! How did you know how excited I would be at this moment?"

Last year Jeremy and she had worked out a plan for their travel. Jeremy would fly in from Miami earlier in the day and wait at the gate area for her plane from Minneapolis to land. Jeremy, faithful to their plan, was easy to spot in his tennis shoes. There he stood tall and slender in his Dockers and khaki jacket, his familiar furrowed look as he scanned the people emerging off the flight. She waited until he spotted her and his expression relaxed into a warm smile of relief and welcome.

Liz ran to his embrace and then stepped back. "Hey you. What's with the tennies? Did you forget it gets cold out east? And it snows!"

"Is that right" he said and then added, "So...what's snow?"

Catching his humor as he took her bag, Liz encouraged him. "It's that rain that solidifies... you know...changes form when temperatures go below thirty. Maybe you've seen some pictures on the December page of your calendar at Miami U. It's called 'winter'!"

He increased his pace and changed the subject. "I called and made reservations for us at the Y in Manhattan, if that's okay."

Liz remembered her stay on her first visit. "That's fine. My little room was cute...it even had a TV! I don't know about you, Jer," she added breathlessly trying to keep up with his long strides, "but I was so happy to get away! This trip was definitely necessary, brother of mine. Do you know what you are? You are a gift...the first of the season!"

They ate at Billy's that evening, after touring mid-town Manhattan in a snow storm. By now the snow had subsided, Jeremy had taken a few hours to dry, and they decided to walk through the neighborhood. Like a "Cheers" bar that sustained the frequent neighborhood clientele, Billy's also provided a "full meal deal experience". They offered a front room with checkered table cloths and a simple menu for the neighbors who frequented, as well as family casual dining for groups, and of course, a bar. In addition for those seeking fine dining and quiet ambiance, there was the rear dining room softened in low lights, heightened with a touch of elegance by white table linens and waiters in white shirts and black vests poised to fill your slightest request. Jeremy had chosen ambiance for their first meal together.

Liz looked around from their table. "Nice...real nice, brother. You spoil me and I wouldn't have it any other way."

"I'm trying to make up for all those times Charles and I ruined your formative years."

"Like the times you wouldn't play "Dolls" and I'd cry to no avail. Eventually I had to give in to strapping on a holster and playing "Cowboys and Indians?" Which reminds me. When I had my first date your tricks reached nothing short of sinister! Before he arrived, you two took the laundry, socks, underwear and, whatever, out of the hamper and hung it around the living room."

"I remember. And do you know why?"

"I cannot think of any reason for being so mean!"

"Our fiendish older brother explained that, since your date was Greek, we should make him feel at home. Charles explained that, in Greece, they hung everything from laundry to sausage inside their homes, right out in the open. True or not, I guess I thought it was rather cool. And, since we didn't have any sausage he convinced me we should hang the laundry. Simple as that...and seeing you running around screaming like a shrew was the height of satisfaction for us. Don't you remember? When we heard the doorbell ring we helped you collect the socks off the lamp shades."

Liz's attempts at taking a sip of her drink failed. Experience taught her the danger of laughing with your mouth full. After she calmed, she continued their humorous replay. I have to admit, my favorite was "head in the box." You'd drape a sheet over the chairs and have me sit so that no one would see me. All they could see was the box on the chairs. With your direction, I practiced pushing my head into the box from below the chairs. The mercurochrome-stained cotton around my neck was a clever touch. What I enjoyed the most was waiting for someone to open the box. Charles had rehearsed it well. I'd open my eyes let my tongue go limp and stared blankly into space. I was only five. It was one of my favorite games. Charles was always the instigator wasn't he? But that doesn't absolve you. No wonder you are so good to me. You owe me."

"Don't push it," he warned as he filled her wine glass.

"May I make a suggestion?"

"Yes, you may. As long as you don't hold me to it".

"Tomorrow can we look for some decent shoes for you to wear?"

Without answering, Jeremy gave their orders and returned the menus to the waiter. That done, he drew his glass to himself, and pondered his beer with the interest of a collector gazing at a piece of art. Liz watched as he sipped it slowly, suspecting conversation would only distract him from savoring the experience.

He looked up. "Decent?" he repeated. "Like opposite of indecent?"

Liz was ready. "No. Instead, how about 'decent' as opposed to freezing your toes off, or worst still, getting frostbite and having them cut off before we have a chance to see Radio City's Christmas Show! That kind of 'decent", and then she added, "Decent as opposed to 'stupid'."

"Aha! What I am hearing you saying, is that I am the only one in Manhattan wearing tennis shoes? That's a stretch you know. We haven't been here long enough to observe all the footwear in the area. Tell you what, sister, if we don't see another person in tennis shoes by tomorrow morning, I may consider your suggestion. That is my condition and I'm sticking to it. And do you know why? You said it! Remember? Because I am a gift, that's why." And all through Jeremy's indignant proclamation he was positioning his tableware in proper formation, straightening his napkin, and continuing his haughty, intellectual airing of grievances, his words becoming more clipped. Liz sat studying him, trying not to stifle the moment by giving into the hilarity that was building inside her waiting for full expression following his performance.

By now their waiter stood with plates in both hands looking at Jeremy as if he had serious doubts about safety on the job. Jeremy's ability to hold a straight face while dealing out humor was the trigger that left those who didn't know him wondering if they should run or play it safe and pretend everything was normal. Suspecting that you are in the presence of an agitated egomaniac is not a pleasant experience. Suddenly, realizing he might be causing a stir, her brother finally gave his face permission to join in the fun. Looking up and laughing, he cleared a space for the awed waiter to place the food in front of them.

"Mmm...delicious!" He met her gaze. It seemed to say. "And I planned it just for you." She and Jeremy had lived apart for so many years and suddenly, she felt sad. Because now, as she returned Jeremy's gaze, it was becoming clear how much pleasure her brother was deriving from Liz's exclamations of gratitude.

As they traveled together, shared meals and long walks Liz's understanding grew to why women were attracted to her brother. Behind that curtain of humor and eccentricity lived a tender soul. She began to suspect her brother lived conscious of the tension caused by this strange coexistence of his vulnerability, with his need for connection. She decided humor was what protected him. His thoughtful pauses the hesitation that preceded his humor, these provided the time needed to appraise a situation and form a response. She began to notice, Jeremy initiated, but very seldom, if ever, interrupted someone while they were speaking. It was as if he were listening with an intensity of focus and concern that encouraged sharing. Then, in his own time, after thoughtful pause, he would enter into the conversation.

Their last day together was spent in downtown Manhattan. Battery Park, Greenwich Village, McSorley's Pub and the campus of New York University, Jeremy's alma mater. The sun was bright and they walked under a cloudless sky As their trek moved into the afternoon Liz noticed Jeremy's mood changing. He became quieter, thoughtful.

"So, what was NYU like?" Her question brought on a strange silence between them that hovered over the day. The timing was off...by about forty years! His stint in the army and their travels had separated them. "But what about the years we shared growing up at home? Why have I waited this long to ask him what his life was like when we were young. Didn't we talk back then...like "how was your day?" Our mom made sure we ate dinner together every evening. The question ignited an astounding revelation! She stopped and looked questioningly at her brother.

Jeremy stopped momentarily and then pulled ahead of her. Liz caught up with him and remained silent as they walked. Jeremy kept his pace as he spoke. "I don't know. I don't remember a lot. It's all a haze."

As Liz walked away from the gate to board her flight back to Minneapolis the next morning, she welcomed the warmth of Jeremy's embrace. She watched as he walked away and watched him turn around to wave to her. And, yes, he was still wearing tennis shoes.

She missed him. And it had only been a few minutes since their parting. She seated herself and rested her head back on the seat. "How can two people live together for years and not really know one another?" Tears stung and she closed her eyes. "Thank you, God. It must be time to ask these questions."

Chapter 3

"The Truth will set you free; but at first, it will make you miserable!"

These were the words Liz read and retained from a poster at a retreat center. They were accompanied by a picture of a rag doll caught in the wringer of an old washing machine. Its message continues as a mantra of solace in difficult times.

Nancy's smiling face was framed in the receptionist window when Liz entered on her morning of return. "Happy New Year! How was your vacation?" Liz breezed by her open door. "Wonderful! I'll tell you all about it at coffee." Nancy always shared pictures after the holidays, and treats which she placed strategically within reach of anyone nearing her little area of hospitality. "See you at ten." Denied instant expose', her voice trailed off as she switched her attention to an incoming call.

Liz opened the drapes in her office and turned to view the stack of papers spilling from her inbox. Retrieving the call slips off the top, she glanced at the callers' names and placed them on her desk in order of priority, with Jen's closest to the top.

That's when she noticed one slip lying on her desk separate from the others. It was from Anne. Liz frowned. Anne's closing comment when they had last met came instantly to mind. "You're hard on men, you know," she had said. This wasn't the first time Liz heard that comment used to describe her.

"I am not hard on men," and then, hearing her words in defense, she added, "Am I?" There was silence. She decided to answer her own question. "Okay, Lizzy, you're mouthing off to everyone else. I just asked you a question". Aware that she was talking out loud to herself boosted her defenses. "No!" she blurted. "No! I like men!" The force of her adamancy toned her down to a whisper... and then a resigned sigh. "I just don't trust them." There it was, out in the open...truth. Again, a statement from her past followed and she repeated, "Once we have been burned in a fire, we instinctively draw back when we smell smoke,"....a man told her this.

"If you ever leave me it will be in a pine box," Ric had warned. They were both tired after months of campaigning. He had decided to run for the Mayor's position. In a small town reputations grow fast and Ric became known for his leadership positions in the Homeowners Association and as an impressive innovator in his work with the county's Civil Defense He was also "six four" with a voice like a ship's horn when he got upset! At this time in memory, his anger was directed at her. "Goodness!" she interrupted herself, "I just realized I've been single longer than I was married. Time has proven the wisdom of that decision."

Glancing at the clock, Liz hurried down to the staff lounge and returned with a cup of coffee. As she closed the door behind her, her eyes came to rest on the statue of St. Joseph on her book shelf. "And you, Joe, you and I have been together through it all. In high school Sister Therese explained one morning St. Joseph was the "patron of a good man." Since this was an all-girls school Liz suspected the message was received by more than just a few as an incentive to hit the local Catholic gift shops The St. Joseph statue she chose was a beautiful carved wooden likeness. She stayed with the memory. "So, where were you during those early years Joe? Sister probably kept you busy with all those Aquinas graduates. I'm glad you finally got to me on the list while I was still young enough to benefit from your special ministry to the lovelorn. The current crop of males in my life are definitely more promising."

She sipped her coffee slowly and allowed herself to follow where memory was leading. Without announcing itself, another image emerged through her reflection....more accurately, six images. They sat dining at a long tressled table in a large dining room. When she was married, that dining room was often the gathering place for quiet meals with family and friends, holiday parties, on many occasions, buffets for people in the community running for political office.

While Ric poured a liqueur, she had begun serving pie. "Apple pie or cherry?" and had just begun to return to the kitchen. An ominous sound jarred her and drew her back into the room. Disbelief caused her clutch the wall for balance. Only then did she realize the sound had been that of shattered glass. Glass! "Glass everywhere! Oh, my God! Strewn on the table, chips on the floor, and as her eyes followed the images in the room she couldn't believe what she was taking in...like a scene in slow motion. She followed the direction of everyone's attention to settle on her husband sitting, unmoving, a look of confusion on his face. Ric sat at the head of the table and in his hand she saw the jagged head of a broken wine bottle. He had smashed the bottle against the edge of the table. And, as glass does, it showered particles in all directions.

Time stalled, sound muted. Seconds passed. Then one tiny voice, slipped through the aftershock. It was their friend, Ellie, holding her hand over her dessert dish as she complained to her husband, "Bob, I'm bleeding!" To which he answered, "Ellie, I told you to order the cherry pie."

That night was among a chain of incidents that had begun to build fear in Liz. In time, she had learned to tame playbacks, and for the most part, after a divorce and therapy, lay these thoughts to rest. Now, sitting at her desk this morning she felt confident in allowing a replay of that incredible night to rise freely.

Still paused, clutching the wall behind her, she knew in an instant that she had to face what she had tried to avoid during those last few years, and that was a growing fear of her husband. He was ill, dangerously ill. Added to this revelation was the fear that she was becoming ill. But, what to do? Who to tell? The night of the shattered glass forced her to act against her fear. Like a burst of light in her brain, what rose up before her was her own guilt for ignoring what was so clear now, and that was the extent of collaborative denial...from everyone, she, their friends, associates! How far we go to enable the facade that keeps reality at bay to insure illusion. Liz will never forget that moment. Rage rose up within her when she listened with horror listening to a friend grasping at comedy to deflect the truth. Accompanied with the emotional shock and an overwhelming shame was the emergence of an aching sadness, Liz recalled. How pathetic to witness a feeble attempt to recover from the assault of another man's hidden demons, unmasked from across the dinner table! The sight of real blood on apple pie brought the curtain down on "make-believe."

The decisions she made that night thrust Liz into the chaos of uncertainty. Every day brought on the choice, "Should I get out of bed, or lie under my bed and hope no one finds me." Liz chuckled recalling those days. It was the 70's, Liz hadn't been out in the professional world for fifteen years. A lot had changed. If she were to chart a new course for her life she had to consult professionals. She applied for a loan at the bank and the banker assured her "Think of it this way. What you used to rely on a husband for, you are simply turning over to your banker." It was 1975. Before the year was up she had sought a banker, a tax consultant, an auto mechanic, a carpenter and a counselor...all males. Who else was there? It was the seventies!

Oh, yes, one female appeared by request, and this was Mavie, the realtor. By first appearance Liz remembers her as "cute and sassy". It only took a few days to uncover "the realtor" in Mavie. She was not only a spark of hope and energy...she was sharp, engaging, cunning on her client's behalf. Mavie made Liz laugh. What fun! However, Liz soon learned that these gifts that made Mavie a business sensation, didn't serve her very well in her personal life, which was a chaotic mess. Thus, at Liz's invitation, she joined her in a support group. One evening she admitted to the group, "My family looked like eight by ten glossies, but we were crazy as coots!" Yes, Mavie was a character and it wasn't long before her breathless quotes were gaining attention in the group. She could describe reality with a limited use of words that touched on truth so humorously, so honestly. Her gift was also her greatest obstacle. Mavie could charm you and at the same time convince herself into believing she was 'working the program' until Liz realized her new friend's stealth at self-delusion mesmerized her away from her own progress. It was very hard to give up the friendship with Mavie. She was so much fun. "Oops! And just thinking about her pulls one away from matters at hand." Liz stood up and stretched. As if programmed into her random thoughts of the past, a song came to her. One she had just heard on the car radio and seemed so appropriate to where she left off in her recollections. So appropriate to life itself she had memorized the lines, "Sometimes, what doesn't kill you, makes you wish you were dead." To which she added, "Don't waste all that good pain!"

The phone rang. Father Kemp's cheerfulness brought her out of her heavy wanderings. "We won't be meeting this morning. I have to visit a family at the hospital. Can we make it this afternoon?" Once established, he quipped, "you can have my brownie." "No," Liz retorted, Nancy will save it for you. You know her. I'll probably get my hand slapped if I reach for it."

Priests. The fact that she served alongside priests these past fifteen years amazed her. One priest came immediately to mind. When she was twenty years old and twenty pounds lighter from stress, her stewardess uniform hung on her like a monk's wrap. Liz was stationed in Miami away from her family in New York. During this time her mom learned of her plans to marry Ric. Thus, she sought counsel from the Church. Liz knew she was breaking her mother's heart long distance. However, the priest who claimed her "running off with a divorced man was a sin of the flesh" did not help the situation. Her father tried by comforting her with "a man who likes hunting and fishing can't be all bad."

As her mother relayed the priest's words over the phone, Liz sunk even deeper into her Irish, Catholic guilt. She decided to fly home to be with her parents at Christmas. And as the stance of pious judgment grew, so did Liz's resentment. It was Christmas week when, in defiance, she made a decision to skip Confession, traditionally a practice before the holy days. Instead, she would shop for some last minute gifts before leaving Manhattan. With this in mind, she began her ascent up the subway stairs.

What happened was so instantaneous it wasn't until later that Liz was able to describe the incident. She remembered looking up the stairway just as two men were coming down from the street above. They were both dressed in long winter coats and hats. One of the men, she recalled later, had his hands in his coat pockets. He suddenly lurched forward and came tumbling down the concrete steps towards Liz. The force of his fall threw her backwards against the persons behind her. "Of course', she recalled, 'he didn't have time to break his fall with his hands!" She heard his head crack against the floor. He lay very still at her feet. His companion thrust her out of the way and began to slap the man's cheeks crying hysterically, "Stan, wake up, wake up!" Liz, already vulnerable from the strain of her personal life, froze on the spot, petrified. Thinking back she concluded that she must have realized, even in shock, that there was some action expected to address this crisis enfolding in front of her. She ran up the steps and yelled to a policeman who was, she explained from an automatic parochial formation, "miraculously standing a few feet away."

So much for shopping. Shaken beyond endurance, tears grew into sobs. She walked blindly forward, groping in her coat for a Kleenex. When next she looked up she blinked to refocus. The big, heavy steel doors, the stone spirals piercing through the snow flakes towards the dusky sky, and steps...this time appearing wider and higher as she was led upward to the entrance of St. Patrick's Cathedral! Before succumbing to exhaustion she grasped the heavy door and pulled it with her remaining strength.

Once inside, she stood very still until her vision adjusted to the dim figures on the aisle. They were standing in silence in a line beside the confessional. Her tensions evaporated as if in response to sitting among the sinners seeking, as she was, to find some peace for the endless inner turmoil from which, it appeared, no one could save them. With that reality prompting despair she rose and entered a "little black box" closest to her. Liz remembers the feeling of being in the dark, embraced, erased, invisible. She tensed slightly with the sound of the small window sliding open. "Bless me Father" she began. To this day Liz has no recollection of her words, only the words spoken in response... the voice that reached out from the darkness. "My God, child! How you have suffered."

That soft voice of compassion was like a flame that cut through the pain frozen inside of her. Then, like gentle drops that escaped slowly from someplace deep, she walked out into the night and away from the Voice, and wept. Only this time her tears felt warm and comforting.

Liz has never had any recollection of going home that evening, nor if that evening prompted the direction and the decisions she was to make a month later. And now, as she sat in her office many years later she knew that she would always remember the one person who understood her pain and did not judge her. "God has a way of reminding us always that, even though people give up on us, and even when we give up on ourselves, we always have a place in God's heart." To her the Voice didn't need a face. To her that evening it was the Voice of God, acknowledging her, holding her, stroking her"

Growing up in the 40's and 50's an Irish Catholic with twelve years of parochial education, Liz faced "catholicity" to her memory, so fearful and rigid that when she fell in love with a divorced man and married him she was programmed to readily accept the shame that accompanied her decision. Shame was like a shawl that she wrapped around her and wore for fifteen years until it began to block the sunlight.

Then, one morning, as she sat in her usual pew at Mass at the furthest end of the church, something extraordinary happened. Or, she corrected, "someone extraordinary happened."

There he was...dressed in a robe bound with a rope sash, wearing sandals on his feet. He moved across the altar as if every step was carefully and joyfully disciplined by a lighter gravity. His eyes burned with intensity and his voice read the scriptures as if it might be his last time to witness. Liz listened and followed his every movement and concluded that day, "This man has been someplace that I have never been!" That was the morning she decided to pursue the "someplace" where she shared with a friend, "we can be recreated into beautiful and confident people like the man on the altar."

Her oldest son, Thomas, was five when he first questioned the presence of priests. Even at a young age, her son's inquisitiveness and intelligence caught the attention of adults. The Franciscans who became acquainted with young Thomas would agree, "He's the one who will be a priest." Thomas always had to ponder and question. At age five, hearing over and over in Sunday religion class how much 'God loves you," Liz guessed he got brave enough one morning, to ask a loaded question. The pastor was mingling with the parishioners after Mass, and her little boy, looked across the parking lot as they drove by, and asked, "Mom, do you mean that man over there loves me even more than you do?" To be mistaken for God must carry a heavy weight!

It took Liz time and maturity before understanding came that priests needed friendships, human interaction, not exclusion from" the rest of us mere mortals." And a child, like Thomas. needed a man, not a god. Liz became convinced that this was the reason Jesus insisted the apostle, Thomas, place his hand into the wounds and see for himself the marks of torture on his human body. My son kept seeking and asking, there again, for someone to stand on his level so he could touch and engage him. Eventually, at age sixteen, he followed his seekings and came to Liz one day to inform her that he was going to be baptized a Jehovah Witness.

At the time Liz was unable to understand and respect her son's need for a male model. It took time to become clear to her. Thomas was too gentle for the overbearing military mentality of his father. And much too perceptive to accept less than his needs craved. Added to this was his persistent search for someone or something to add meaning to his life after his parent's divorce. She was able to understand how " sitting at the feet of the teacher" as displayed in paintings of Jesus, in humble form, such as a parent, an uncle, grandpa, or a lay elder was far more real to a child than growing up at the foot of an altar separating him from a vested image towering magnificently over his littleness. And so, by age thirteen Thomas decided his six foot-four inch dad in military uniform was just about as towering as he was able to endure without the presence of wise human models of solid and simple daily example. Thus, Thomas made his decision. Liz remembers that day he came home and made his announcement. "Naturally," she reflected, "I was full of guilt over my child abandoning the faith of his Irish ancestors and, especially the part I was sure that I played in it with my frantic wanderings."

"Given years to assess it in the light of God's wisdom and my limitations," Liz mused to herself. "Thomas has found a place of fulfillment that requires no explanation. He is ministering in the missionary field with Russian speaking people, preaching in fluent Russian, living in distant countries subject to mold, and fleas, and rats, and government corruption and "he is so fully alive and happy, he lights up a room." Liz rose from her chair and stretched again, long and contently, as she contemplated how rich her life had become through the seekings of her little boy to find God.

Gaining from her plunge into a world much larger than her imaginings and meeting people who appeared as fellow seekers and guides, life became one huge adventure for Liz. During her initial experiences with single parenthood, she once lamented to a priest aged and wiser than she, "Was it presumptuous on my part? I always thought that God would answer my prayers and bless my marriage." The priest answered, "He has." Liz let herself be silent. She understood. As if Gibran's words came to life, she repeated, "the same cup that holds our pain also holds our joy". She swiveled her chair around to face the sunlight coming through the window. "So this is what life is about. Thank you, God, for the children who lead us...who share their innocence and joy with us, until we adults who think we know it all, begin to listen and blossom along with them. Liz grew to treasure her oldest daughter's words on a family retreat. "Thank you, Mom, for growing up with us."

Chapter 4

"Hello there. Is anybody home!" Liz started as a knock sounded and Fr. Paul's tall frame appeared and filled up the doorway. "Did you get my memo?"

Liz reached for the pink slips and rustled through the papers. When she was sure her brain clicked into present time, she swung her chair around, and faced the figure blocking the light from the hallway. Like a jolt from an ignition, her eyes sparked into full alert at his sudden appearance.

"Yes, I'm sure this is it...oops! She reached for his memo and then followed its descent as it came to rest under her desk."

"Never mind," he assured her, "We can discuss it in my office."

He shut the door behind them and offered her a seat. "I was giving you time to adjust after your trip. I suspected your body might be here, but I can see your brain hasn't caught up with you yet? How was your trip?"

They compared their holiday events, Paul describing ice fishing up at a family cabin.

"Have you ever been ice fishing?" he asked.

"Once," she answered quickly. "I was four months pregnant and didn't know ice houses do not have bathroom facilities...at least, not back then. The only suggestion the three men present came up with was for me to squat outside on the ice with only a blanket protecting me from a north wind. When I returned from an unforgettable ice-chilling experience I remember gazing down at this hot cup of steaming coffee they offered me, wishing it were a tub full so I could soak in it! That experience of helpless embarrassment taught me never to walk on ice larger than an ice cube and that's only when I happen to drop one on the kitchen floor while mixing a drink."

Father Paul's hardy chuckle startled her. He held up his coffee cup and showed his amusement. "I'll drink to that." Although, being an avid fisherman, I don't need much coaxing to "walk on water," provided it's frozen, that is. Soon it became clear he was waiting for Nancy to bring coffee. "Whew...this is going to be a long session," Liz thought.

"I wanted you to know that our Hmong family showed up for the feast of St. Nicolas."

"Really! How exciting. Did they stay for the gifts?"

"They did," and she noticed his smug look. Mai Lee brought her mother and two sisters." Liz waited without interrupting. He continued, "You're the Social Justice advocate. I would like you to think about engaging this family in parish life at St. Joseph's. They seem to be looking for a connection. I don't know. It's more of a feeling. What do you know about Hmong?"

"Well, this is going somewhere exciting" Liz thought, allowing herself a moment to catch the arrows of enlistment heading her way. "From conversations with Hmong and reading about their culture, I know that they are mountain people, people of the land...farmers who left persecution in China only to find themselves in a war when the Americans enlisted their help against the Communists in Vietnam. They live in tight community, peaceful, hard workers, uprooted from Laos, massacred in droves after the Americans pulled out, sought safety in Thailand, only to be evicted and sent here to America. As of this year there is approximately forty thousand Hmong in the twin cities, and growing. When I inquired about their religious beliefs an elder explained they don't have a religion as we describe in our culture. Instead, they worship their ancestors, and, if I understand correctly, they call upon their presence when celebrating life or grieving their dead.

"Are any Catholic?" He reached for his coffee cup, saw that it was empty, and sat back in his chair listening with interest.

"According to our Pastoral Council and certain members on our staff," she began, trying not to sound insipid... Hmong are not Catholic. But I discovered by checking with the diocese that we have a small Hmong Catholic community forming right here in the city. And," Liz held her breath and took her time. She was beginning to enjoy their conversation. "What I found out from perusing through the local news, is that at least some of the Hmong in our immediate area have been welcomed by a church a few blocks away. And the church, which is Episcopal, may be bilingual. Her last statement caused Fr. Paul's eyebrows to rise up his forehead with the speed of a desktop and then settle again over his eyes, which had left their focus on her as he stared over her head. He didn't fool her. Fr. Paul was conjuring a strategy behind his distant stare. She waited for a sign of his return to the conversation. It appeared in the form of inquiry. "Bilingual? Are you saying they may have a Hmong priest, or perhaps an Anglo priest who is bilingual? Hmm, or, perhaps they may even be just renting space to the Hmong." Liz used his speculations to bide time for choosing her answers.

Fr. Paul showed his middle age. His hair was receding and a little pouch was creeping over his beltline. And, she concluded, his years, as well as those in the priesthood, taught him to listen well and to ponder, as he seemed to be doing now as she waited. Overall, she had noticed, he never seemed prone towards the extremes...either amazement or discouragement. "Cool," she had to admit in her summary. If he did react, it was instantaneous and over with, as she reminded herself of the rapid rise and fall of his eyebrows when she said the word "Episcopal." Right now Liz was caught on the edge as she tried to anticipate where the conversation was leading.

A knock interrupted them. Nancy entered, tray in hand, and announced, "I arranged some holiday treats on a plate. I thought you might like to have some with your coffee." Fr. Paul looked up seeming instantly pleased for the break and, as if they had some ongoing secret conspiracy, responded, "Nancy, how did you know I had my eyes on those brownies since yesterday." After an exchange of mutual relishment, Nancy excused herself and closed the door. Liz had come to respect Nancy. No, this was not because of Nancy's will power over the frost-glazed delicacies she had to handle every day. "No, no, no!" Liz mused. "It was her victory over the temptations, "Liz suspected, " that surely plague her daily in her position of confidante to news or gossip, as well as her passion for gathering secrets and firsthand information." In spite of this, never once, had Liz caught her with her ear against a door. Her discipline was exemplary. With this observation of a lighter note, Liz forced her attention back to business.

"I don't know all the answers to your questions. I do know when I drive by their parish, their worship sign announces services in Hmong, and then in English below that."

"Hmm," he responded followed by a nod of his head. Then, like someone privy to a revelation, Fr. Paul gestured forcefully, a brownie in hand, directing his next statement with such clarity of purpose it unnerved her.

"You will find out. Just let me know when you can visit the Episcopal church this week. And maybe Anne can go with you."

His next comment surprised her. "What drew you to St. Joseph's?" He followed his question by reaching for the pot and filling his coffee cup. Then he settled back into his chair with, she thought, "the air of a therapist."

Liz straightened, clinging to the comfort of the warm cup in her hand, letting her memory form her response. "Because it is a small parish, and an urban ministry. I grew up in urban settings."

"And, what was it that you were seeking when you answered our ad?"

"Simplicity, I guess, and diversity. Before I was hired, I drove through the area of little houses, tree-lined streets, small lots and fenced yards, some even sporting antique clothes lines. I was pulled into the simple scenes and back into time. It made me yearn for an earlier time when, I think we were kinder, or at least, more content. And diversity? When I was growing up my family was submerged into a melting pot. The Jews had the fish marts and delis, the Irish were the "cops," the barbers were Italian, and the local grocery store was owned by this sweet little man, John, who was Armenian. Why he wound up in the north Bronx I never thought to ask. We just took differences for granted and by all appearances, we thrived on diversity."

Liz ended her avalanche of words abruptly. Father Paul stared into his cup, not appearing anxious to interrupt.

"Okay, Liz. You've tested long enough. Time to dive in!" And feeling the swoosh of air around her head, she leaned into her subject and gave it all she had. What the heck! "I'll either cut a smooth swath and surface like a champion, or I'll knock myself out and sink to the bottom."

"The community around St Joseph's that first day was a pleasant trip back to a time I thought no longer existed. I was right. Now that I am a part of it I have come to the realization that my first impression was colored by wishful fantasy. And since I've touched reality, I share the pressures of change with everyone here. At the same time I struggle with what I see as a unanimous resistance. Like, "if we ignore it, it will go away."

Like it or not, our new neighbors are changing the dynamics of our little community, and it's not necessarily a bad thing. It is just pushing us into reevaluating how St. Joseph's is going to serve the community that surrounds it...and I mean the community that is...not the community that was. We aren't in the fifties, or even the seventies. Back then culturally divided parishes worked. We had a Polish church, an Irish/Italian church, a French church and so on. Now, St. Joseph's has to decide whether we can go on being our neat little Irish/Italian church. This generation doesn't come in neat little social packages of the fifties. And, what about the Hmong and the other new immigrants...the Asians, the Spanish, the Indians, the Somalis? America is becoming global. The world is becoming global. And in a smaller sense, St. Joseph's is resting right in a center of action. As I see it, it is becoming imperative that we begin to address this migration, integration, (she ran out of words) situation, whatever..." catching her breath, Liz continued, "in our own parish, and accept our Christian responsibilities to widen our mission. To me, this is a call to move beyond our lot line and prepare to serve the growing needs that, I'm sure we will find as we reach out. Evangelization for us as Roman Catholics is becoming relevant to the times, and too obvious to ignore any longer.

Fr. Paul remained graciously attentive even when Liz suggested closure by folding into her chair and appearing to struggle for fresh oxygen.

"Are you finished?" he asked, breaking his silence.

"Yes...and relieved. And, as we say in the groups, "thank you for listening."

Father Paul sighed. "Liz, I appreciate what you said. Once more, I agree with you."

"You do?"

"Yes. And I admire your gift of vision."

"Is that what it is? Is this what afflicts me...I mean...am I suffering from "vision"...or more accurately, "visionitis"? It sounds like a "bug," and in that case, I wish it would infect the staff so we can get this show on the go! Maybe I'm dumb, but I really don't know what your appreciation and admiration looks like. It gets lost in the maze of silence leveled at me over the table at staff meetings.

"Haven't I supported you?"

Paul had this way of squinting and pursing his lips that reminded Liz of her high school teacher waiting for her to pass in her test paper? Which was always accompanied by the pressure to have the correct answers.

"Yes...she began, and then hesitated. But I'm never sure. You are good at moving us on when the air clogs with opposition, but when it is just murky I have trouble finding your position, Okay. I admit the time we approached the Liturgy Committee for permission for placing social issues into the basket to be brought up with the gifts during Mass. Did you have something to do with their final approval?"

"A ha." His response was brief but Liz knew she got the first question correct. Next?

"And the group that appeared before the City Council to appeal the change in bus routes so that our older members could continue to be picked up at their usual corner. Yes, we won that. Oh, yes, I remember, you came with us."

"A ha!" Paul's responses were becoming more insistent. "And, young lady, this conjures up all kinds of friction which I endured because I pushed for the cultural brunches. And one event plays in my brain, bringing with it the pain of the Vietnamese converging en masse on our little church and cooking in our kitchen that did not accommodate full cooking facilities. This alone left me vulnerable to admonishment for ignoring fire rules. I still shudder when I recall the ugly looks from our administrator as the aromas of that meal filled the church during my homily!"

Images of those proud people dressed in their native styles walking through the tables, looking so pleased as the diners greeted each one with enthusiasm and applause, came dancing back into Liz's memory. O, what a grand idea that was! She realized Father Paul's recall was slightly different from hers. Thus, easing back the pleasure she felt, she put on her straightest face. "I'm sorry. But don't you think, notwithstanding a few problems, that the brunches were fantastic!? Oops!" A sudden flash of discomfort interrupted her confidence.

"I just remembered my meeting with the priest who filled in when you took a vacation last summer."

Paul stopped squinting and began drumming his fingers on the desk blotter.

"I simply asked him if it would be ok with him if I gave the homily for the next week's readings." Paul's responded with a frown. "But, Paul, that was when the staff were occasionally giving homilies. And the priest did say Yes."

"He did?"

"Sort of reluctantly", she admitted. On second thought, he may have been in shock." Liz restrained a giggle remembering the old priest's reaction. "As it turned out you had commissioned a missionary to speak from the pulpit that next week. Sooo, neither of us gave the homily."

The force of his laugh jolted his head forward. "Saved by divine intervention!" He collected himself and put on his "vested look," Liz called it. "It means, 'keep quiet and listen'...gospel time...attention!" And Liz settled back.

Fr. Paul's words were always simple, easy to understand words that draw you in with a warmth of compassion, but not to lull you, because behind those words rumbled a quiet authority that one doesn't dare to ignore.

Paul stood up began to move around the room. "Liz McKenna, you are a gifted person. This is the reason I chose you for a position on staff. You are creative, visionary, compassionate, articulate...that's enough," he cautioned himself and then continued. "I can define each one of you on staff and give each of you reasons why you are qualified to be here. I chose each of you. That's my blessing. And that's my dilemma. My responsibility is keeping you all supported and encouraged in your individual ministries, and, along with supporting you, I have to keep you working together...a team.

"I may be able to venture into your projections as you envision what may be good for St. Joseph's but a vision is only as good as the people who are following it and working within it. We grow into the vision together. That's the struggle. Because it is normal that each of us comes here every morning with our own perspectives and personal expectations. That's where patience comes in, perseverance, focusing on the possibilities, anticipating and encouraging dialogue as something new emerges and begins to take form. And, each time you, or I, or someone on staff has a plan, places an idea on the table, we enter the struggle again, mull over, stretch the imagination, review our resources and most important, we pray. Prayer allows that space for God to complete what God has begun My job is to take what each of you offers and keep you moving forward as one body...oiled and operative, huh?"

Paul came to a standstill by his chair and sat down. He leaned forward and looked expectantly at her. "Do you understand?" he asked.

Liz closed her eyes briefly to slow the reeling in her head. "Yes...yes I do." She was back in the class room again only this was the oral test. "You are reminding me', she began, "that... we are all gifted. And that the staff is responsible to make these gifts accessible to one another. It is not my vision." she continued, "It is God's vision. Which means, allowing time and space for each of us to enter the vision, which requires our accepting this will not be within the same time frame. It's becoming clear at this moment, that I must listen more, for instance, to the practical elements of progress... maybe like finances, resources and, whatever it is I seem to be overlooking in my zeal. Liz was plainly used up...overwhelmed with the clarity of Fr. Paul's description of moving ahead on team effort, as well as being forced at this moment, to face the difficulties she unknowingly may be causing with her impatience and demands.

When she paused in her concentration and looked up Father Paul seemed lost in his own thoughts. As if returning from another world with his message clear and affirmed, "the Boss" rose up from his chair and half smiling, approached her. "Liz, I know I gave you a lot to think about, but, please I don't want you ever to lose your fervor, your humor and your spontaneity. We need these gifts. The Church needs these gifts!"

He opened the door for her to exit. And then turned to her and announced, "You know, you are really hard on me."

Liz knew she looked like someone had just hit her on the head with a water balloon.

Chapter 5

"Like the wailing of a distant train captured and placed to murmur in my heart..."

...Liz sought things contemporarily for their style and convenience. However, she acknowledged within herself a need for balance, free expression, which she discovered, was a style referred to as "eclectic." It became her measuring sense as she decorated a new home. Liz was a mixture of sophistication and simplicity. She never understood the mix of seeming opposites within her but found completeness in meeting their needs. As a result, her homes eventually became a haven for the splash of fad, mingled with the calming effects of timeless treasures of the past. Every shopping venture left her anticipating the rush of color in a pillow or throw, or that unique design of a window covering, that tweaked her creativity. However she still claimed antique shopping as her favorite "hobby." Most times she made no purchases; but hovered over racks of collectors' displays. Like the scratches on silver and the beauty of old wood that drew from her a strange reverence, she sought and savored the timeworn for its luster and durability.

Dusk was settling in as she drove up the alley leading to her house and braked as the garage door responded to the click of her remote Two years earlier, when she was scanning the neighborhood for a house, the ideal would have been to choose one with an attached garage. However, emotions ruled in her decision to surrender this feature to the charms of an early 1920's bungalow a mile from her ministry position at St. Joseph's Church. Ignoring her realtor's concerns over its obvious flaws, she became enamored by its black walnut cabinets, stone fireplace, arched dining room entry, along with an enclosed front porch "crying out for wicker and lemonade in crystal pitchers." In addition, a major selling point for a single, working woman was the size of the lot. Later she would boast, "It only takes fifteen minutes to mow my front lawn."

A year into light renovation, her respect for the little house moved up another notch. During a ceiling repair, a carpenter discovered newspapers dated just months before the stock market "Crash" of 1929. "It gave me a strange feeling of foreboding that seems to still hang in the atmosphere in the denials of our own times. When I read through the luxuries touted in those ads in 1929," she had shared with staff over coffee the next morning, "and the casual lifestyles of prosperity that hid the fragile realities, I felt sad. It's like squandering foresight! As if, instead, we keep trying to reverse the truth with the power of the remote. For instance, replaying a disaster movie over and over hoping for a different ending. How did we get so oblivious!" Liz, aware of her natural incline towards heavy reflection, especially on social issues, moved her thoughts on to recollections of a more pleasurable experience, that of the first morning in her old "new house."

She remembered listening to the sounds of coffee seeping into the pot and filling the kitchen with what she called, "the aroma of home and hospitality. There's something about perking that first pot in a new house that transforms a dwelling place into home." She poured herself a cup and breathed in the scent of fresh coffee beans mingling warm with her sense of contentment as she walked through the rooms slowly, making note of the paint peeling on the window sills and several water marks on the ceilings, the clouded window panes crying for a squeegee and ammonia. The work to be done didn't bother her. There was nothing that demanded more than she was capable of, or she assured herself, "that couldn't be turned over to a professional...with time...within budget. "Why rationalize any further? You were hooked the first day, Liz, when you slowed the car to survey this charming old place. It nestled in humble welcome, set back from the sidewalk among two old oak trees." The attraction grew more insistent. It reappeared as a presence that seemed to resonate from inside the walls during a walkthrough. This was the house, she knew, that was promising her an end to her wanderings of the last five years from one apartment to another, part-time assignments, school schedules and tight budgets.

On her first early rising in her new home the far-off sound of timeless assurance wailed its welcome on the still morning air. A sound she would become used to as the trains from the local depot wailed and whistled their endless journeys. A sound that linked her to her own journey, as well as to all those just like herself, who were seeking a claim of their own, to arrive somewhere, to rest at a destination and experience the contentment she was enjoying at this moment. The wails of distant sounds, like train whistles...or the sad, slow tunes of a tenor sax being carried in the night in the midnight hours. "Soul music, sounds that call us out to join with our own souls. Sounds that echo back longings that lie tamed within us until stirred. These are the longings that remain undaunted, constant and insatiable. It's like having terminal homesickness," she whispered as she listened. Without warning "like ghosts commissioned to remind us of our incompleteness, an incompleteness that seems to stay with us in spite of a lifetime of homecomings."

Once again, bothered by the depth of her reflections, Liz turned her thoughts to the present and walked out her back door into the winter chill. The effect was instant freeze. However, she braced herself and ran to inspect close-up what she would refer to later as "my prized antique"...an old fashioned close line! She was quickly reminded of the lunacy of standing in the cold without her coat and gloves, and reversed her steps towards the house. Gathering her senses she returned to gazing at the clothesline, only this time, through the kitchen window. A statement she had read from a recent magazine came to mind. "Today', the article stated, "people are spending thousands of dollars to make their houses look like grandma's"

As the years past, Liz's bungalow had not disappointed her, nor had she reneged on her commitment to restore its original beauty as best she could. "The old girl hugs me when I walk in at night," she would say.

After her meeting with Father Paul this morning and getting an affirmative from Anne who promptly put their visit to the Episcopal church on her calendar, Liz spent the day playing "catch-up." She was tired and "needed a hug," she mused as she began her ritual of dinner prep. She poured herself a glass of wine, which she balanced as she settled into her big couch buried in pillows, and dialed Jen's number. "Hi! How's Lucy doing?" she inquired of Jen who had offered to keep Liz's little dachshund while she was on vacation.

"Since she's licked the skin off everyone's faces, I'd say she is having the best time of any of us. What do you give that dog...happy pills?"

"I know. She's always been like that. If dogs are extroverts, Lucy tops the charts."

"How was New York?"

"Good! I even took some pictures. I'll have them developed for our next visit, which I hope will be soon. "How's your week"? Without waiting for an answer, Liz continued, "It's your birthday! Why don't I treat you to a dinner at my place on Wednesday. It's my day off."

"Agreed! And I'll bring Miss Congeniality with me."

"Okay then'...and with a familiar hesitancy she added, ' barring any emergency,"

Jen exhaled deep into the phone. "What would that be? Aside from a death, funeral or sick call, a parishioner being evicted or burned out of their home, what possibly could go wrong?" Jen knew. She worked in hospice.

"I've already got it on the calendar. It's called living your faith. Hey, Jen, mind if I ask you a question?"

"What do you think? I find your questions very interesting...even when I don't have an answer it doesn't seem to discourage you, which I appreciate. Besides, just the question alone sometimes keeps me going for days. You know, I mumble to myself and people ask why I keep walking around shaking my head."

"Quit it! I'm serious."

"I'm sorry. Ask away."

"Am I hard on men?" Liz kept a hold on the phone and waited. Jen took a while.

"Well, if you are, they don't seem to mind it. Even the gay guys seem to thrive on your abuse. Oops! I meant "attention." No. Seriously, I don't know you as an abusive person...not at all. But then, I don't work with you. Best you ask at work. I joked about the gays because a certain night a few years ago instantly came to my mind. Remember those two gay guys we were introduced to at a dinner one night? That night is just another embarrassing experience that is etched into my conscious recall. There you were, the three of you laughing, and I sat listening trying to still the panic in my chest."

"Oh, yeah. In fact, there were several occasions that come to mind where we attended together and, as you describe, I was clueless...unless of course, you're exaggerating my naiveté", she kidded. "However,' Liz retraced, " remembering your agitation, I would be safe in saying, the reason for those enforced bathroom breaks is that you became so incensed and embarrassed, you used a legitimate excuse as a substitute for screaming and lunging at me in public." Liz was having fun. She hoped Jen was, too. With that slight pause of friendly concern she returned to the subject.

"I don't even remember where we were that evening or why," she continued. "I do remember those two men that joined us at the table. And I also remember how relaxed it was to be in the company of two men who were not putting the moves on us. Ha! Now I know why! Then, of course, I was just annoyed that you excused both of us right in the middle of some great conversation. Until we were in the ladies room, that is, where you informed me that I had been saying some things that could be misunderstood..."offensive"...you called it. You flipped me on the shoulder and blurted, "Do you know what you are saying!"

"Yes!" Jen jumped in on the other end of the line. "Yes! I'm sitting listening, knowing you're clueless, and I'm getting more upset. Later, however, I reconsidered. I should have let you go on blissfully because, when we returned, you appeared so demure I was getting sick. I was relieved when they excused themselves to go to a party. That wasn't the first time I felt like your mother."

"How about rephrasing that using 'big sister' instead." Liz didn't have to wait for a reaction.

Jen responded immediately, "And how about the fact that your being older makes you the big sister? I'm younger, remember? I can't help it if I'm smarter."

"I hadn't noticed," Liz teased.

"And, since you always laugh at your own jokes, I'm glad to see that you catch the humor in mine once in a while. Go eat your dinner. I'll talk to you before Wednesday. And, please, no more questions. I've had my prescribed dose of hilarity for today."

"Love you," Liz countered.

"Love you...call me."

The oven timer sounded. Liz, her fatigue somewhat lifted by their conversation, reluctantly rose out of the plush feel of pillows and hurried to the kitchen.

Chapter 6

"Morning comes on slowly,
my mind clears.
Sun rises,
warms away my fears.
I rise
to meet the day.
Life is true,
life will bless me.
this I pray...

Shafts of morning light moved across the blinds. The slap of the newspaper against the front steps broke through her dream and she smiled. Liz remembered past years of struggle. Affording the daily newspaper represented the rewards of perseverance, as well as the pride one feels with re-entry into mainstream. "Mainstream!" Liz bolted upright in the bed. "I'm meeting Anne to make our visit to the Reverend Alice at the Episcopal church!" Her body tensed and then relaxed back onto her pillow as she recalled her initial phone conversation with Alice, the priest. "Not Reverend, not Father, nor Mother nor Sister nor Brother," she reflected. When the Pastor's phone was answered the voice was definitely female. This was followed by the Reverend's introduction, "This is Alice Spencer-Lamb." No title and no insistence upon recognition of her position. "How refreshing," she murmured.

The meeting at St. Nicholas to research Hmong culture and religion was scheduled for early morning. Being pressured by Father Paul to team with Anne on what Liz had planned as a solo endeavor was adding to her stress. She quickly brought to mind their last conversation and was encouraged. Observing for years Anne's zealous focus on her ministry to youth, Liz had convinced herself that Anne, too, may have been coerced, and "certainly had other things planned for today that had priority over learning about Hmong culture." In addition, she, herself, was not prepared to lead an interview of any substance on the subject. The spontaneous scheduling, brought on by Father Paul's insistence, and accompanied by her lack of preparation, added to her discomfort. Liz sat up and crawled to the edge of her bed where she carefully balanced herself to light the candle on the small table she called her prayer table. "Candle- gazing," as she referred to it, quieted her. The sound of birds filtered through as chorus grew. "Now why couldn't people wake up like that? Birds can balance on a branch the size of a twig and not miss a note!"

Liz finished morning prayer and blew out her candles. Her walk to the kitchen to fill her cup from her auto-timed pot impressed on her how programmed her morning ritual had become. When moving into the unfamiliar, she took comfort in the taste and aroma of that first sip of caffeine. Her vague memories of Episcopal encounters plagued her.. Encounters, of course, provided by her Anglo friend, Jen. Her amusement grew as she recalled her first Communion Service when she visited Jen's church. Early in the liturgy the images on the alter, that of the vested men, drew her interest. "They are married! Married!" At first this reality enthralled her, the images provoking an array of thoughts to which she impishly allowed full reign. "Wow! Hidden under that vestment is a family man! A father in his sweats who may have waited that mornings to see the children off on the school bus, or a coach for his boy's Little League, a parent committed to diaper changes. Beneath those sacramental robes stands just an ordinary guy carrying his wife's shopping list in his pocket!" Startled by a sudden rustle of movement, she was saved that day from the brink of sacrilegious ravings by the rustle of the congregation rising to sing.

"Having personal experiences through my friendship with Jen, hardly meets the criteria for being informed about my subject...nor calming the quaking curiosity I'm beginning to muster. She swung her feet over the bed and announced to the space around her, "Okay, Lizzie, buck up ole girl. Put on your 'cheeky face.' Still your Roman palpitations. The Brits await you."

As Anne and Liz entered, the priest was giving the final blessing after Holy Communion. "A female priest!" Liz glanced quickly at her notes to ensure the introduction of the name she wrote in her notes...Alice Spencer-Lamb. "And she is married!" Looking up to share this revelation, she faced Anne whose countenance wore a tight frown, softened only by a smile that appeared to linger undecided. Liz forced herself to concentrate on the smile. She whispered, "Isn't this exciting?" Anne's response did little to reassure her. "For whom?" she retorted lightly.

Their efforts to blend in with the congregation failed as people gave them inquisitive glances. And it seemed to draw the Reverend Alice in their direction. "Which one of you is Liz McKenna?" she asked, extending her hand. Liz extended hers and hoped the warmth in her response acknowledged that of the Reverend's. Introductions followed. "And this is Anne Shay, the Director of Religious Education at St. Joseph's Church."

Alice Spencer-Lamb was a tall woman of middle fifties, perhaps, and very slender as she stepped from the sacristy unvested. Neatly coifed, un-jeweled and feminine in her simple fashion, she appeared pleased, her greeting cheerful. "It was kind of you to meet with us," Liz heard herself responding, "and we will show our appreciation by trying to make the most of our time." This serene woman, with a voice that resonated a quiet authority, led them to a large room furnished with a long table... obviously for staff meetings. As she directed them to the chairs she asked if they would like something to drink. Liz seated herself and, looking up, was encouraged to discover by Alice's gaze, that this gracious woman was giving them her full attention. For a moment there was silence. It seemed to fill the room and settle on them. Afterwards, Liz described the moment as "the opportunity for the Holy Spirit to join them at the table."

An hour and some minutes later Liz sat silently behind the wheel of her car. Anne was the first to speak. "I am glad I came this morning." Her comment drew Liz's curiosity. With keys still in her hand, she settled back in the driver's seat hoping to encourage Anne into further conversation. "Anne, I am so relieved to hear you say that. My whole mood depressed this morning thinking you were pressured into accompanying me."

Anne hesitated... "If truth be told, at first I resisted. Later my curiosity began to build. You're the one with vision and crazy enough to stick your neck out. I decided you probably needed some support. I'm farm- steady and you're city-sparkle. I'm beginning to think we're a good mix. And have you considered that, perhaps, our differences percolate the necessary ingredient to..."

Liz stayed quiet waiting. "What is the word I'm looking for?" Anne struggled, and then blurted, "conspire!" Liz turned and looked at her in disbelief. "Conspire? Like in conspiracy? Anne Shea, did I hear you right?" Flustered by her own admission, Anne retracted quickly, "No no..." and then started laughing, amused at her choice of words. Quickly recovered, she continued, "What I mean is together," we might just have the necessary skills to assist the Staff and the Council to facilitate a common vision for St. Joseph's." Liz kept her eyes on her, nodding, until Anne paused and become silent.

Seconds passed and when it seemed Anne, satisfied she had succeeded in talking both of them into fresh perspective, changed the subject "As to a previous comment regarding my accompanying you today? I don't have to be coerced, or directed or motivated by any other means, into supporting you. I want St. Joseph's parish to become the best it can be. This is only going to happen if we work together. I struggle, too, to support Staff, practice patience with the Council and still focus on being accountable to my ministry to the children. It hurts me that you appear to overlook my cooperation with many of your projections.

"Whoa!" Liz interrupted her. She felt cold. It was getting very cold in the car. She put the keys into the ignition and started the engine. Her thoughts revved, as if the engine and she were tweaked simultaneously. "Whoa! Do you know what I'm hearing? Your words just then had a familiar ring. Father Paul, using different words recently to relay to me a similar message... and that is, my total immersion into moving our parish into a vision blinds me to those who are trying to convey their openness and encouragement I am confronted again, chastened and humbled". Liz relaxed and let her head fall to her chest. "What can I say?" She brought her hand up to her forehead to dramatize her pain. I am embarrassed and contrite."

"Okay, Sarah Heartburn," Anne quipped, "are you ready for a recap. Liz sat up straight in a show of immediate attention. "What a woman!" Anne exclaimed. The chain of events leading to the Reverend... starting with she being invited to be Assistant Pastor of this little church in Minnesota after meeting the Pastor on his only visit to the seminary. And being led to accept because it offered an opportunity to return to her roots! Events just don't fall into place like that every day. Meeting her for the first time was impressive enough ...well, my admiration grew listening to the events that followed her becoming Pastor."

"You mean the Bishops notice of closure?" Liz interrupted. She remembered reading somewhere notice of the church's demise due to a drop in attendance and, of course, finances. I was impressed with what transpired next. It sounded almost biblical, prophetic, in the way the characters in the follow-up story, each played a role in opening a new vision.

Anne was following Liz's summary. "What was that? Coincidence? I mean the Catholic church on the other side of town losing its priest in the same time frame? Who was that who stated, "coincidence is God remaining anonymous."

"Act Two," Liz interjected enthusiastically. "Enter the Catholic deacon's wife, knowing of St. Nicholas' plight, suggesting the Hmong consider a new "home" for their community in the struggling Episcopal church. How unexpected was that? The Hmong members who were welcomed originally by the Anglo's numbered in the seventies. It was their arrival that saved the little church from closure! Ta da! The end. Curtain comes down. Applause follows."

Anne's expression tickled Liz. "She always put on that face when it was obvious" Liz thought, "my comments were pushing us over the top." Easing up on the drama, she continued. "Yes, you were impressed! I was knocked over when I asked Reverend Alice who conducted the Communion Service for the Hmong and she explained there were two services, one for the Anglo member, one for the Hmong. Weren't you impressed when I asked who led the Hmong service and Alice answered, "I do" ...well, that brought me to my feet!"

"After you were knocked over," Anne's humorous comebacks were becoming more frequent as their friendship grew. Liz paused, reconsidered a retort and proceeded undaunted. "She not only opened their community to strangers of another culture, but she honored that commitment by learning their language! She was so patient explaining so many things, like how the Hmong didn't have a language until a Jesuit priest in the missions taught them. So much of her story was told with such a spirit of respect and care for the needs of both congregations." Liz finally closed with the emphatic statement that was to turn into a mantra for both of them in the weeks to come. "It was meant to be!"

Liz pulled the car away from the curb and drove toward St. Joseph's. Anne was quiet. Liz heard her murmur the words that carried on her breath as if to seal the bond of mutual conclusion, "It was meant to be." Liz parked the car and they sat in silence. Anne spoke first, "What are you going to tell Father Paul?"

Liz looked wistfully into the distance. It had begun to snow. "That's why you are so calm, Anne, and enjoy your ministry. You minister to the children. Our Church loves the children. Adults cause too many problems. And this is why I live in a constant state of frustration." Liz pushed the car door open. Let's go inside. And pray The Boss is doing hospital visits this afternoon, or attending a deanery meeting. If so, we might be able to conspire on an exit plan before his returns."

Chapter 7

Liz checked her notes written at 2 A.M. and quickened her morning routine so that she could arrive at the church early. Coffee in hand she peeked into Anne's office and was relieved to find her looking alert and enjoying a cup. "Good morning! Are you sufficiently caffeinated to have a serious discussion before we meet with the "padre"? Anne looked up and rolled her eyes. "Oh," she groaned, "it's you." Then she smiled and added, "Good idea. Sit down."

Liz sat and jumped right in. "We covered our first responses in the car yesterday, so we won't rehash. We don't have time. And so, need I ask? You have given thought to what it would mean to accept a Hmong child into our community?" Liz leaned her head backwards and focused on the ceiling for a moment and then brought down her questioning gaze directly at Anne.

"I need both of us to think hard. What will it mean to the staff and to our parish to open the doors to a one Hmong family? And I emphasize "family" because what we've learned from other parishes is that one turns into many. Not that it's bad, understand, but its implications hit me last night and I really had to ask myself, "Is this what St. Joseph's needs at this time? I don't know."

Anne turned from Liz and stared down at a paper on her desk. "I'm thinking." Noticing the time, Liz waited impatiently. "Okay!" Anne's face softened with that familiar smile that always preceded thoughtful responses. "Honest!" she blurted and then eased back.

"This may sound selfish on my part, but I'm thinking of the boy, too. I ask myself, "Am I prepared to welcome him into a comfortable faith experience considering he will be the only Hmong with all white, English-speaking children? And what about you, the crusader for community outreach? If it should appear necessary, are you prepared to learn Hmong?

"No," retorted Liz. "Are you kidding?" Anne's smile got broader.

"I know what you're saying, Anne, and I've prepared myself for inquisition. I didn't stay up half the night convicted of my hypocrisy under pressure to arrive this morning without a plan. In fact, I almost predicted your question. Because, Anne," and Liz found herself welcoming their banter, "I anticipated your level-headed and practical approach. "No!" and Liz repeated again with emphasis. "No! Learning to speak Hmong is the furthest thing from my mind at present! It would be an all-consuming commitment on my part. Not to mention I failed Spanish in high school. Oh, yes, and just imagine how the Parish Council would receive the news that we are welcoming the Hmong! They already think I am plotting to overthrow them! With their current suspicions directed at me, I 'm not ready to push the button that will start a war."

Anne rested her head on her arm, just taking it all in as if, Liz noted, she was actually enjoying this grand recital before staging it for their priest. Liz waited. "I'm impressed," said Anne, seeming to enjoy the challenge. This is when she delivered the hook. "And now that we have come to a meeting of the minds on this, how do we work it into our presentation to Father Paul, which is, by the way, in about fifteen minutes?"

Those fifteen minutes proved fleeting. They were still hanging out their case for a first airing as they hurried down the hall. As expected, Father Paul had a pot of coffee and his favorite doughnuts on the side table. He was already helping himself as they entered. Liz passed on the doughnuts and gripped her coffee cup to anchor herself. The combination of fatigue and tension left her unsettled...irritated. She tried breathing slower and realized "The Boss" had just asked her a question.

Collecting herself, she passed him a sheet of paper that summarized their meeting with Reverend Alice and settled back while he perused it. Liz didn't look at Anne. Anne was a person of many subtle expressions. She didn't dare to leave herself open to the one her associate may be communicating at this moment.

Paul perused the paper and placed it down on his desk and commented, "The little I was able to absorb at first glance tells me you had a very interesting meeting yesterday. So, now, are you prepared to fill in the blanks? That is, of course, any ideas or conclusions each of you may have reached in the last twenty hours...time, may I say, you were left free from my meddling."

It was Anne who spoke first. Relieved, Liz settled back in her chair. "Paul," she began with a reference that revealed their years of working together. "I wish you had been with us to meet the Reverend." Expressions of awe and pleasure flowed from her and drew the padre's interest immediately. After which she was "grateful for the opportunity she was given to visit such a simple and beautiful church that compares with St. Joseph's." Liz shifted forward to encourage her to continue. "When Anne rises to the moment, she can sure pour it on!" Liz mused silently.

Father Paul motioned for a break to refill his coffee. He walked pensively back and took his seat. Liz began,

"Now that Anne and I have formed and presented our mutual concerns for the Hmong family, I have a huge concern of my own that has plagued me the past few hours. And that is Reverend Alice's revealing the loss of almost half of their congregation after accepting the Hmong." Her emotions built with the contradictions of the words she was about to speak. She steadied herself to give force to her words of admission.

"I know I have pushed social agenda's and justice issues. I've exhausted efforts to move our parish out into the larger community, to accept the cultural changes in our neighborhood, to consider God's call to embrace new neighbors, including the immigrants." Liz measured each word. "Like the curtain going up on reality, everything became clear to me just as I walked in. And that is, I know now, in my enthusiasm to push forward what I believe is good for St. Joseph's, I missed a vital piece of the possible consequences. I never considered the price...that is, what would be the cost for moving ahead on this. St. Nicholas lost almost half their congregation!

So, this being cold reality, and while already feeling the pain of being accused of hypocrisy, are we ready to take such a risk? Are we called to such a risk? Excuse me for interjecting a personal observation here, but I don't think this staunch Irish, Italian community is, or maybe ever will be, ready to embrace peoples of other cultures. At least not yet in my estimation. A community who, up to this time, can't seem to muster a small group to venture out into the surrounding area to meet new neighbors...who, by the way, are mostly white second or third generation American. To be drawn to ponder so much by the innocent inquiry of a little Hmong boy has forced me...and I suspect, you to reconsider, and to question our mission at this time. Perhaps the whole thing has turned up the obvious. That it may be as simple as I have been suggesting, an outreach to the new young residents moving in down the street.

Liz caught her breath and dropped eye contact, an effort to gain reprieve from further thought. With as much professional discipline she could muster she closed with..." (There goes Paul's brow again... rising from concentration to heights of anticipation) Spurred alive again by the humor in noting this, an idea came instantly to close with a quote from him. "A vision does not belong to one person. To become a reality, a vision requires all of us working together. She ended with "quote, unquote" and allowed herself the relief that follows concession.

Silence resounded, broken eventually by Father Paul. He cleared his throat, rose from his chair, raised his hands and began a resounding applause. "Bravo! I am taking you both to lunch." Liz and Anne looked at one another and when they looked back at Paul, he was grinning. "Now," he added, we have to come up with a plan for this family. God is calling them through this little boy."

Lix stood and looked in Ann's direction. "Anne, thank you for seeing this through with me. I, for one, have gained so much from your participation and your sharing our meeting with the Reverend

Alice" (She knew Anne would blush. It's difficult enough to compliment her in private, but even more difficult to have someone witness her moment in the sun.") Liz learned over the years to go light with accolades so as not to embarrass this person who was destined to become a treasured friend.

"So, now," Liz began upon awareness that she still held their attention.

My plan is to meet with Mai Lee and her family this week. After which, if it is acceptable to both of you, I will bring them to meet the Reverend Alice Spencer-Lamb. If either one of you wishes to accompany me, all the better. Alice will know what to do. Her community will welcome them enthusiastically, I'm sure. And we? We will be able to visit back and forth and,"...she paused mid-sentence..."once again give thanks and praise to the Spirit for always making sense out of confusion. Which proves again what the contemplatives say, "God works best in the dark."

Father Paul stood up. His groan as he stretched expressed his relief and a tone of satisfaction that assured Liz and Anne the meeting was adjourned. As they passed him in the doorway he asked, "Lunch? And I think we should order some wine to celebrate liberation! ... of St. Joseph's, St. Nicholas', and the little Hmong family up the street!"

Chapter 8

Winter, I've had it!
Ice-chunky roads,
last Fall's corpses
creeping from crusted
dirty snow.
I know,
"Pray for serenity."
But, Lord, today
preserve my sanity,
and indulge me
my list of vendetta.
Tomorrow, you'll see.
I'll be feeling much betta.'

Like the turning of the page memory ceased and, instead, music and the sound of singing broke through and relocated Liz into the present moment. Her eyes opened wide as she realized somewhere in the maze of her thoughtful wanderings she had dozed off and tripped into the past. Reentering her immediate surroundings, she became aware of the noon Mass in process at St. Patrick's Cathedral in New York City.

Looking around she surveyed her space from the pew and wasn't surprised when she met the gaze of the piercing, pain-racked eyes of The Lady in the icon hanging in the alcove beside her. Once a week, for years, she visited and lit candles at the altar of Our Lady of Czestochowa. As a child of a parochial past she was taught by the Dominican nuns to honor Mary, the Blessed Mother. However, the years brought distance between her and Mary as she became more and more aware in the experience of her powerlessness in a male world, Liz suspects she eventually became impatient with Mary and turned her attention, instead, to her Son, Jesus, who seemed to have privy to the ultimate power and, from all accounts, was more than willing to share it with everyone regardless of circumstance, status or gender.

And this distancing continued until a visit to a Benedictine Monestary one day introduced her to The Lady of Czestochowa. Searching over the offerings in the gift shop during lunch break, Liz paused before an icon of beautiful tragic figure, a woman holding a child. Familiar, but yet, this woman was scarred and her gaze seared through Liz and bonded them instantly. The icon, she learned, remains one of the oldest icons of the Blessed Mother in the world. Legend has it that St. Luke painted it on a cypress tabletop in Nazareth in 326 A.D. It was transported to Poland years later as part of a dowry and suffered considerable damage during the war in 1430. In the moment Liz's eyes met the eyes of Luke's "Mary" or "Mary of Poland," it was like all her experiences were affirmed, at the same time her justifications challenged.

The pain of her son Thomas's accident rose up within her with a fresh vengeance remembering when he was seventeen and hit cycling home from his job at the market, Crushing pain, like the car that threw him from his bike and across the hood of an oncoming car, his head shattering its windshield. When her son lay dying, hung like a puppet on tubes, Liz faced her utter powerlessness to restore life to her beautiful boy. These feelings brought her for the first time in many years to a reimaging of Mary, but not as this passive, bowed figure of serenity, but the Mary of the Pieta she had seen in Rome. Mother Mary, holding her lifeless son. Liz knows her prayers to Mary brought Thomas out of his coma and back to life with no apparent lingering effects, except for a broken eardrum.

However, not until the Mary of Czestochowa, Poland's Mary, looked out at her with eyes slit and intense on the edge of her endurance, lips tight with resolve and her face marred by a scar of a double gash on her cheek, (claimed to have happened in Poland's war but remain in spite of efforts to remove them during the restoration)...no, not until this Mary looked out at her did Liz know that Mary had flesh, and was real, and she understood and lived the experience, not only for Liz, but for every female that endured. For every woman, every mother exposed to suffering by the very fact of her vulnerability and her faithfulness to vision and birth in all form for Life's continuance. Not until then did Liz fold, her resistance evaporating, her anger affirmed, her love returned.

Liz listened to the music, and once again became a victim to our Lady's piercing gaze. She covered her face and hoped the distress stirring inside of her was not disturbing the serenity of her surroundings.

"Oh," the revived Liz's exasperation growing, "this was not the end!" Months later, when she inquired at the Cathedral's gift shop where she could find pictures of The Lady of Czestochowa...after exhausting her search of the saints on the display, the sales person left the counter and pointed to a card in one of the slots. The woman must have noticed her expression and asked, "Isn't that the saint you were looking for?"

Liz held the plastic card in her hand and couldn't believe what she was seeing! "They," "Whomever" authorized to desecrate the holy to uphold sanctity, had Botoxed Mary's face, gave her an eye lift, and replaced her simple head cloth with a crown of "golden gadgets"!

It has been years. Liz is still trying to recover. "Maybe I never will," she would whisper to herself and, again she would visit the altar at St. Patrick's to share freely her raging frustrations with the "real Mary" in the icon before her, whom Liz has come to trust, the Mary who understands with a piercing wordless look. What words can describe a mother's pain? Why do we try to hush birth screams? Why can't men allow a woman to simply be who she is. She was never meant to compensate, nor compete, only to compliment, and isn't this the wisdom behind differences? We need feminine images that inspire us to be real. Not someone else's doctored version of ourselves. After a few moments of quiet consideration, she told herself her thoughts, "Yes, she said to herself, "We women are guilty, too. Why are romance novels so popular except to give the female the license to create the male image to fit her own ego needs."

Yes, she whispered to herself, I guess I am hard on men. And now I think I know why. I don't want men to be afraid to be honest. Because then they feel free to insult me by their attempts to mold me into other than who I am in order to validate their egos. I have worked too many years enduring the pain of self-disclosure to allow someone else to reimage me so that they can escape their own soul work.

She looked up at the beautiful tragic Mary of Czestochowa, and down at the plastic card she took from her purse, and lamented, the only prevailing reality in social and institutional systems, and these are designer fashions, intrusive cosmetics, and cultures of the modern world with their incessant preoccupation with the feminine image. Liz caught her breath and voiced her sadness, "And look beautiful Lady. Look what they did to you!"

As the large metal doors of the Cathedral lumbered shut behind her she could hear those precious words echoing and then fading, "Lamb of God, who takes away the sins of the world; have mercy on us."

It had begun to snow. A few blocks further and she found herself outside a store with signs, "Grand Opening" and realized it must be the new store written up in this morning's news. The displays featured styles and merchandise from Japan. A quick tour of three floors convinced her that the Japanese were noticeably light and tiny. The tops were too fitting, the pants too short and the workers too fast. "Well, she remonstrated, "what did you expect? Not only have the years added pounds, balanced your taste to a middle ground of "classy to casual," but slowed you down and made you totally resolute in your aversion to fads. Resistance especially directed to men in business suits wearing trousers that look like they are caste-downs from their little brothers!"

A few blocks and she reached Saks. Following instructions, she took the elevator to the fourth level, which the salesperson explained, was "Home Decorating and Gifts" . She browsed through looking for kitchen items and met a woman looking as perplexed as she. The woman walked up with what appeared to be a tablecloth and asked, "Would you know where I can find napkins. I'm trying to match up for a dinner I'm having." Liz resonated, "'I've spent the last five minutes looking for placemats. Doesn't Saks carry plain ole kitchen and dinner ware? I've shopped Saks for kitchen and table linens for years". A quick check with a badged employee confirmed that Saks no longer handled kitchenware." On the way down in the elevator Liz peeked out at the floors. Doors popped open revealing, Designer Shoes and Purses, Designer Clothes, Designer Jewelry and Cosmetics. Cubicles and counters announced them by name in large letters...Calvin Klein, Christian Dior, and some with names that needed linguistic talent depending upon the designer's country of origin. Women, by quick reference through the sliding door at each floor, seemed to outnumber men, and their movements resembling that of bees, buzzing from place to place, probably employees on lunch breaks. Liz wondered what kind of a salary supported a designer market. "And," she questioned, "doesn't anyone cook anymore?"

The day became too long. The snow, like the day, heavy and intimidating. Liz walked to a bus stop and waited in a biting wind. The world seemed strange, unfeeling, wired. As she settled into a seat by the window she found herself looking forward to a cup of tea and a nap.

Chapter 9

"Hi, Mom. How are you?" It was Clare calling from Minnesota. "Have you thought about returning to the Midwest lately?"

"Lately? No. But, if you keep asking, one of these times I may come to my senses and reply with a "yes.""

"You know how persistent we get as Christmas moves closer, Clare continued. As eldest child I have been commissioned by my three siblings to put pressure on their mother once more. As you know from your past visits we do concede to your wishes to return to urbanity. But then, if you've been noticing, we rally everyone to line up at the airport to wave farewell. That way, your family instructed me to tell you, your last view of us weighs you with guilt so heavy they tag you as "excess baggage.""

Silence followed. "Now that I've exhausted my humor, I think you should know this year, Jen and her family are visiting from Michigan during Christmas week." Clare's announcement brought instant response from Liz. Her "Yes!" pealed into the phone assuring Clare she had delivered the hook. She knew her announcement would be difficult for her mother to refuse. "Yes," Liz repeated, "Yes! I promise. I will check flights to Minnesota for the holidays and get back to you."

"We're holding you to it, Mom. And, keep practicing those yes's Mom. We'll talk again soon."

"Jen...dear Jen." It had been years since they had seen one another. Liz was still ministering at St. Joseph's. August came and it was a few days before Jen's birthday. Liz had invited her over for dinner. Anticipating their usual ritual, Liz decided to drive into town for a bottle of brandy so they could celebrate the occasion with their favorite cocktail.

The morning was clear, fresh and bright as she drove across town, her purchases securely bagged on the floor beside her. She merged to the left lane to avoid construction barriers blocking her way. Liz slowed as she noticed the car in front of her signaling a left hand turn. She braked and waited for the oncoming traffic to give clearance to the driver ahead of her. Her attention moved up to the rear view mirror. In that same moment, her vision blurred. Her body shifted violently and lurched forward. Propelled suddenly from behind, her car hit an unyielding force and that is when she heard the sound of crunching mettle. Simultaneously, her head bounced backwards as it jarred against the windshield. Dazed, Liz sat in the settling quiet. A fleeting moment of regret for not buckling her seat belt seeped into her confused thoughts. A painful throb in her head began to synchronize in time with the beats of her heart. There was silence all around her, broken only by those throbbing beats and then a loud moan, which she realized, was hers.

The next moment brought movement and people's voices as a man stuck his head through the open window on the driver's side. "Hey in there. Are you okay?"

Liz couldn't immediately answer. She felt normal, except for the ache intensifying in her head. The next visitor to her window wore a uniform. He instructed her to remain seated. While the shadow forms moved about outside, a slow pass of her hand across her forehead disturbed a film of what appeared to be dust speckles that danced across her vision. No, she decided, it wasn't dandruff from a dislocated hairdo. It was glass! Glass so fine that it rained like talcum. She checked again. No blood...just a rough surface spreading across her forehead and releasing tiny particles as she ran her hand over it.

After a visit to Urgent Care, x-rays, and a brief interview with a doctor who suggested two ibuprofen, Liz was released from the hospital later that afternoon. Her poor little Cooper, pounded into drivability by some benevolent employee of the corner gas station, awaited her as she walked across the parking lot. The sight of her little car waiting wounded and forlorn was the tipping point. Liz stood still and foraged in her purse for a Kleenex. "Dumb," she whispered. The word muffled by sniffles. "Damn!" she corrected with vengeance.

"Dinner will be a little late," Liz explained with, she thought, a steadiness of tone improvised to cover her emotions.

"What's wrong?" was Jen's immediate reply.

"What? Does something have to be wrong? The table is set, the glasses are iced, the chicken is spiced and..." Liz abandoned her attempts at calm. Jen obviously spent too many hours with terminal and overwhelmed patience to ignore the obvious tremors emanating from her attempts at composer.

"I was in an accident." Liz held the moment before Jen could begin her interrogation. "It wasn't serious," she assured, but her emotions returned to plague her. At least I look a heck of a lot better than my Cooper. Poor baby...all bent and crippled...besides the cost and...

Jen interrupted. "Liz, how did this happen?"

Liz's anger resurfaced for the replay. "According to the police some guy in a white pickup truck revved out of the corner gas station behind us, cleared the construction barriers and then realized the two cars he was approaching were both stopped waiting at a left-hand turn signal. Evidently his speed was accelerated beyond control and he plowed into the back of my car. This caused the chain reaction that propelled my car into the rear of the car in front of me"

Jen's impatience showed when Liz took a breath. "Then...then what?" Urged on, Liz continued. My head hit the windshield. I'm fine. Although I have a slight headache."

"Honey," Jen's plaintive response followed. "I'm coming right over."

"No!" Liz was surprised how forceful her voice sounded to her after surviving a near death experience. "No! No! You just come over as we planned. I don't want you getting all upset on your birthday. Everything is prepared. I'll see you at six. And, Liz smiled delivering her spontaneous exit line, "And, Jen, God is good. The brandy made it through intact."

"Happy Birthday," Liz toasted when they were comfortably settled with iced glasses in hand.

"And here's to car insurance and a long life," added her friend with a smile.

"We've celebrated a lot of birthdays, haven't we, you and I, and the children. Jen's voice dropped and her head tilted thoughtfully. "We've had a good life. And we've always ended up laughing. I'm sure it's how we survive." She looked up and, focusing her laser look onto Liz, asked, "Why pain?"

Liz' stared back, feeling like their cruise ship was returning to port. "On your birthday you are entitled. I guess that includes asking questions. But why plummet us into the depths before I've had a chance to take my first sip?" Noticing Jen's persistent look and posture, Liz restrained further attempts at humor.

"What are you asking?"

Jen seemed content that she had captured Liz's attention. Her first sip brought instant response. "Mmmm," she raised her gaze in delight and then settled again into her subject. "Why do we have pain? Why does it have to be?"

"Oh…" Liz followed her back, and pondered the question. "If you asked the Wise Man that question, he would answer "Why not?" Noting Jen's seriousness she quickly inserted, "I read that in a book. To be honest, I needed a few moments to prepare my poor inflamed brain cells for the plunge into a discussion on pain Meeting Jen's eyes still focused on her in anticipation, Liz decided to give in and to follow her friend into the deep.

Jen was certainly well versed on the subject of pain, struggling many years with back problems, in addition to raising a terminally ill child and surviving a divorce. These were just a few tragic realities Liz knew about through their friendship.

"Pain, huh? What a remarkable birthday theme. Puts one in a real celebratory mood." Liz paused then to communicate her return to seriousness before continuing. Well, I would say that pain must be a very important ingredient for living a full and meaningful life, and that is because God did not exclude it from words to live by. And

Christ certainly personified the reality of suffering as well as the accompanying perseverance needed to build character. Not to mention we Christians glorifying the cross as a sign of hope. Jesus' sacrifice would prove senseless if pain were irrelevant. I think it was Gibran who wrote, "The same cup that holds our pain also holds our joy." And then Liz added, "If you will indulge me my references. That is because I know by experience that this statement to be true. Persevering through a divorce and all its struggles not only for survival but for liberation for our whole family, opened huge wounds that took years to heal. I used to say, "It isn't the healing that hurts as much as the surgery."

"Surgery?" Jen interrupted.

"Yes. This is when and with the support of people who keep assuring you they love you, you're called to cut deep into your pride in order to discover the causes of your misery. Once enlightened, love demands we guide our children out of their sufferings. Which for most were caused by the poor choices we made. Remember the words of Jesus, "Woe to you who scandalize my little ones." Pain is, I think, God trying to get our attention. That I think was C. S. Lewis." Liz rebounded. Okay! How about this? You tell me, if pain is irrelevant and has no purpose except to add misery to misery, then why are we sitting here today undefeated by it and celebrating life? And Liz interjected, "Although I would prefer singing right now as opposed to opening and peering into old wounds." Oh, well...

"And about the cup that holds our pain also holding our joy? When Clare was ready, she fell in love. The day my oldest child got married, and I watched my beautiful daughter take her place at the altar, all the pain of the past seemed to dissolve. Pain had cut deep and for so long but now, suddenly, this moment became the time of filling! And, Jen, I experienced a joy that felt like the top of my head came off!"

Jen listened, her eyes seeming to rest and then wander off to some far off place. Liz paused and Jen began to speak. "Like birthing"...she murmured thoughtfully. "The pain of birth. Why do we choose it over and over. Because we come to know and anticipate the joy that comes with the birth of a brand new baby…new life! The joy erases the memories of birthing pain. In fact pain is the motivation that drives us to cooperate with the process. To resist just intensifies the pain and prolongs the natural process. Like life itself, sometimes we have to be encouraged to stay with the pain, to follow it like working with the natural push of our muscles in birth and …" Jen's voice deepened and became soft in the presence of revelation. The baby! New Life! Joy? Oh, my God! The sound of that baby's first cry! Yes! The joy to hold this tiny form and to gaze at its sweet face for the first time."

Liz raised her glass. "Life! You explained life! Follow the pain it brings me out to someplace I needed to be…new and fresh. Resist pain and I prolong the maturing process. And, now that I think of it, what about that little baby? Poor thing. He or she breaks out into this bright, noisy room after listening to its mother screaming and swearing and pushing him out of this nice little warm chamber into what must appear to be pandemonium. And what is its first reaction? He feels the pain of a strange and threatening world and starts to wail his displeasure. And what is our response? Are we upset? No. The baby is in pain, obviously. Instead, we're relieved and rejoicing that our baby is alive and healthy. Who can figure? Maybe that's why life is described as the agony and the ecstasy by some who live on a higher plain than we do.

"I remember Robert Schuller on T.V. one morning quoting Jesus' teaching about trusting God through the changes and upheavals of life. He asked, "And how do the lilies grow, that neither toil nor spin?" He waited to give the intended effect. And then he answered his own question. "With friction! How does all life begin, grow and come to fruition? With friction!" If I remember, Gibran also wrote something like, "Pain is the breaking open of the seeds of our understanding." We could follow our theme into seeds and fertilization and, how babies are made …" Liz raised her glass with a twinkle of delight, looked at Jen and asked, "How are babies made? With friction!"

Liz's Irish genes danced front and center and urged her on. Without checking herself she rose to the sounds of her own voice, "Here's to friction!" Her laughter rippled as she raised her glass high. "I'll drink to friction and fruition! Now, can we lighten up?"

Jen stood up suddenly and held up her glass. "To friction!" You nut! You put something in this drink. A potion, right?"

"Yes! The label read, "one drop opens secrets in the brain. Two drops and you feel no pain."

"Hold that thought, Liz asked as she left to check the oven. On her return she filled their glasses and settled again. That's when it happened. Jen noticed. "What's wrong?"

"I can't move my neck. In fact I think my whole body is sprained."

Jen moved quickly across the room and took the glass out of Liz's hand. "I know what's happening. And I know what you need, too. Listen. Go into the bedroom and take off all your clothes. I am going to run a hot bath for you.

Mesmerized by pain and Jen's officious orders, Liz walked slowly down the hall to carry out instructions.

"Oh, this feels so good," Liz exhaled as she sunk into the tub. "Wow! I think I will live to tell about this night. And I'll add what happens to a good Irish Catholic girl when she turns her thoughts to sex."

Jen appeared again in the doorway with a tray. "Sit up," she instructed like head nurse. Liz was not prepared when Jen placed her dinner on a tray-stand over her bare belly and then, once stabilized, set her full wine glass on the tub ledge beside her. "I can't believe this. What are you doing? Oh, this is ..." and then she knew she had no words to adequately describe the actions unfolding before her.

Soon Jen reappeared with her own dinner tray and took her place on the closed toilet seat. As she positioned herself and glanced over at Liz the comedy in their situation hit. Liz watched as Jen slowly balanced her wine glass and, assured preparations were complete, began to laugh. "Now, are we ready to sing?" Liz had been too immersed in the strangeness of it all to sense the humor until spurred on by Jen's release. Stirred suddenly out of a trance-like concentration, she held tight to her tray and, together, they let themselves enjoy a breakthrough in dining experience.

Later, Liz listened to Jen moving about the kitchen. She sat on her bed welcoming the comfort of warm flannel against her body from the pajamas Jen insisted she put on. Flannel in August? She felt the giggles rising. An eruption of non-stoppable giggles poured out of her. When the phone rang she sat still trying to squelch the attack. With her hand over her mouth she quieted to listen to Jen's voice.

"Yes, Father Paul, I will tell Liz you called. Oh, she's fine. Right now she is in bed. What's that? No, no pain. Right now she is feeling no pain." Liz went mute and fell back onto her pillow. With a final exhale of surrender, she mouthed "Amen" before giving in to complete exhaustion. "No pain," she sang softly as this soft, comforting cloud enveloped and freed her body right down to the lightness in her toes.

Chapter 10

Jen had stayed the night. Her note greeted Liz as she followed the aroma of fresh coffee and peered around the doorway of the kitchen. The note read, "Your breakfast plate is in the refrig. I'll call you later." The phone rang. It was Nancy.

"Hi! Good morning! Fr. Paul left me a note on my desk after his hospital calls last night. We're all wondering how you are."

Liz was soothed by the concern in her voice. "I'm grateful. At least I feel a heck of a lot better than I did last night. A pickup truck rammed me yesterday and threw me into the windshield. It must be, I hope, my prayer life because I survived the impact with no more than a headache and a sprained finger. How's that for drama?"

"What a disappointment you'll be when I tell your story at coffee break. I am assuming you're not coming in this morning. In that case, do I have permission to add a little excitement to your bland account...maybe just a titch."

"Oh, don't worry about that. When I relate the whole story it will exceed your expectations. And, I promise, it may even satisfy your taste for the bizarre. Is there anything pressing that would drag me in today? Otherwise, I'll rest."

"Not really," assured Nancy, letting her sentence drift.

Liz responded, "Hey there. What secrets are you hiding behind your stealthy little pauses today?"

"Okay," she relented all too quickly. There is a note on your desk. Flo wants you to call her as soon as you are able. She sounded upset."

"If Flo is upset, it's serious. I'll call her from home. Greet everyone for me."

If ever there was a pair that worked and played together, kindred, generous spirits, it was Florence and Evelyn, the widows of St. Joseph's. They met when Evelyn, a young widow, reached out to Florence after her husband died. They have been inseparable ever since. When one is present, you know the other is somewhere in close proximity. Over the years, the congregation began referring to them affectionately as "Ev and Flo."

They were unified and constant in their commitments, their engagement in social issues, and their enthusiasm for new ideas, even seeming to relish the challenges. Ev and Flo, though different in personality, shared the same unwavering honesty. If you wanted a straight answer, you asked one or the other. Ev was playful and extroverted. Flo was the introvert, an insatiable reader and fact-finder. Even as a staff person one was never guaranteed support at first hearing. For this reason, having them present at planning meetings was sometimes an agonizing process for those anxious for rapid conclusions. The positive side of the patience demanded was that whatever Ev and Flo eventually decided was good for St. Joseph's they entered into with energy that surprised even the staunchest of the younger members.

"Hi, Flo! I hear you called the parish and left a message for me."

"Yes, I have to speak with you about Ralph."

"Ralph? Ralph! Flo, are you dating?"

"Oh, no." Flo chuckled and her tone lightened. "Ralph is my dog."

Her clarification brought more confusion, as Liz struggled for a response. "Your dog? Ah, I see. You're upset about your dog? What's wrong with Ralph?"

Flo inhaled and let her breath out slowly into the phone.

"Ralph is dying. He's sick. The doctor says he has cancer. I know he's old, but I didn't expect he'd be leaving me so soon. We've been together for ten years."

Liz got caught up in Flo's emotion. She remembered the pain of losing her beloved terrier last year. Her grief was intense. She spoke carefully."

"Flo, what is it that I can do for you at this time?"

"Well, you know what we always do when someone is sick. We pray for them. And sometimes we gather to pray together with them.

"Flo, are you asking for a healing service for a pet...a dog? I apologize...**your** dog. And, may I ask, how many are you thinking will be present at your service for Ralph?" As she waited for a response Liz felt herself being drawn into what she later described as "a conspiracy of compassion."

"Oh, just a few special people, like Ev and my daughter and maybe one or two from our Monday morning Bible Study."

Liz's ambivalence returned. How did she once describe that term...mixed emotions? Later in research, Webster's version proved more accurate. She felt herself "attracted, drawn in, but, at the same time, cautious and ..."

"Are you crazy!" a voice inside her screamed, which she recognized immediately. She took a moment to consider and felt the spontaneous thrust of adventure lighting cells in her brain like sparkles of moon light on fresh snow. Slowly she took in all in and heard Anne's words, "It was meant to be."

"Yes! Yes! What an idea...a burst of life...fresh theology unfolding from a small group of faithful supplicants. "Flo, may I have today to pray about this? Your words have really touched me deeply. I will call you first thing in the morning. Okay?"

With the disconnect still buzzing in her ears her focus became fixed on the coffee pot. With an urgency that revealed her reliance on caffeine, she grabbed a cup and poured, inhaling deeply relying on just the aroma to add the mental clarity to meet the task. "Oh, Lord, here we go again. I hope Fr. Paul won't have a problem with this. Or maybe he would, that is, if he thought it would cause some to question "But," she assured herself, "if Flo asked him, he'd accommodate her I'm sure. How could he refuse? "

Her answer to her own question came quickly as indecision evaporated. "Or, perhaps this is why Flo asked me instead of Fr. Paul."

As Liz walked into St. Joseph's lobby the next morning strains of "Nora Jones" mellowed their way out to the lobby. Nancy saw her and aborted her CD on the spot.

"Well, how are you this morning? I knew you would be here today because Flo called and said she was going to bring Ralph to church for a healing service. Liz, Liz, Liz..! "And Nancy's volume grew with the humor intended as she delivered her lines. "How far will you go? Next we'll be announcing pet services in our weekly bulletins. Are you going to make house calls, too?"

"Liz received the humor with relief and relaxed into the chair by her desk. "I couldn't say no to Flo...oops, doesn't that have a poetic ring to it? No to Flo," she repeated. "Now, admit it, could you? Her beloved Ralph is dying. Doesn't compassion compel an affirmative response?"

Nancy's face brightened and she leaned into Liz, "Can I come, too?"

As they worked on prayers and other sacred components, Nancy grew pensive. Liz noticed. "Is something wrong?" Nancy answered a phone call and then returned to their conversation. "Do animals have souls?" It didn't take Liz but a second to answer. "I don't know." Not wanting to become entangled in further discussion, she gathered her candles and prayer sheets and, before exiting, turned and added, "I'm sorry you can't make it to the service. If I get some calls just tell them I'll get back to later this afternoon. And, yes, if Fr. Paul asks tell him I'm meeting with some people in church and will check in later. I won't be long. Oh," she hesitated, "and when you have a few hours we'll talk about the soul." She held Nancy's gaze for a moment before turning in the direction of the small chapel."

Ralph was a handsome dog. The grey flecking his black head and wisping down around his ears and cheeks added dignity to his large stature. He lumbered into the church slowly, keeping time with Flo's cautious steps. He greeted everyone with a nod to pats on his head, wagging a happy tail as the five women cooed and fussed over him. Ralph proved amiable and receptive as he followed Flo's directions and stood quietly in place...a real gentleman.

Under the watchful presence of the Sacred Heart on a ledge overhead, Liz lit the ritual candle while, as she always did, invoking the presence of the Holy Spirit. When the time came for those present to intercede, they followed Liz's lead and laid hands on Ralph. As if already feeling the gentle power invoked on his behalf, Ralph lay down and closed his eyes, listening with head raised attentively. Liz prayed:

> Father, we are here today to express our gratitude for Ralph, your precious creature who has brought unconditional love and companionship to Flo for all these years. Now he is ill and in need of your healing.

We gather to ask you, O Divine Healer and Lord of loving compassion for physical healing for Ralph. At the same time, we ask for grace for Flo to be at peace as she accepts your holy will. As you support and strengthen her to companion Ralph in his needs, fill with joy their time together for the rest of Ralph's days.

Flo, not much for hugs, bent forward and whispered in her ear, "Bless you as we have all been blessed today, especially dear Ralph. I think he already has a fresh spring in his step." As car doors slammed in the parking lot behind her and words of parting reached her ears, Liz knelt and slowly released her thoughts until she felt ready to surrender the rest of her day," and then she added, "as well as the impending reactions that may arise as a result of the holy impulses of my nature. What can I say, Jesus? Call it intuition. Call it "following my gifts." Whatever the source, I just can't help myself."

Later that evening Liz sat reading. The dachshund with the cheerful personality, snuggled close in the chair. Lucy's shift in position and some strange force emanated a pull that eventually disrupted Liz's concentration. Liz let her book rest in her lap and looked into Lucy's eyes. Those eyes...looking with... with what? Love? Steady, pure... grateful? What? It seemed in that moment as if Lucy's entire being was fused with an energy that warmed the space between them. Liz's response was immediate and familiar as she recalled times during Mass, she became conscious of some quiet force prompting her to meet the unwavering bright eyes of an infant studying her from the pew in front. Steady and focused like a ray of "knowing" directly at her. The experience so personal, seemingly unnoticed by those around them.

Running her hand over Lucy's soft furry body she wondered for a moment, "Who is inside? Who are you who looks out at me with such affirmation, such clarity? Soulful, yes, soulful...the only word that rises to the occasion, to describe the look that asks only to experience me, to share a moment...as if this creature, in innocence, knows something about me and yearns to share it. Is innocence capable of seeing through to a secret place within each of us that holds the truth of our need for...for what? What do we receive from our pets that is so desperate that we surround ourselves with these simple creatures and trade after-hour cocktails with associates for the joy of coming home to a squirming fur and sloppy kisses. Love... is this what Lucy is showing me that compels me to attention. I cannot deny it Lucy. My cover, which I manage to utilize quite efficiently in the professional world, is stripped away in an instant by your sweet gaze of unconditional, adoring love.

Do you have a soul? Yes. Is it the same as mine? I don't know. But one thing's is for sure. You have privy to things that I can't even perceive."

Liz paused to consider her last statement. Providing a reprieve from word kill, which Lucy quickly took advantage of. She moved into position, leash gripped between her teeth, tail swooping the air, waiting. "There is an obvious language barrier that puts limits on communications between the species" concluded Liz. And added as she rose from the chair, "But dogs seem to find ways to overcome it. Between props and body language you come across loud and clear, Lucy girl."

With the first inhale of fresh evening air, Liz's whole being filled with energy. She followed the path of stars overhead and then moved down the street in sync with Lucy's gait. Something inside of her suddenly expanded and she felt joy. Turning the corner they met the moon cresting on the edges of trees along the park. "My soul doth magnify the Lord" burst from her. "Beautiful! "Can you feel it, Lucy? I know you do. It's our souls!!"

Chapter 11

"My name is Michelle, she said
How soft that sounds, I thought
"Like her. I liked it
Michelle, so soft,
like angel... spirit...light...
or any other wafting thing,
awesomely grand,
when captured in flight.
Passing through our lives,
sometimes all too fleeting,
but so stirring, as she was to me
that memorable night."

The night Michelle died Liz McKenna discovered her soul.

Over the years, as Liz was active in her Catholic faith, the soul was never a topic of mainline discussion. Not even an issue considered for prime time, as if, after taking time to reconsider, Liz thought, "It," the soul that is, was mentioned more frequently in religious context. Otherwise, "It" appeared in conversation to describe a deeper experience from music, art, or a literary piece that inspired or awakened the "unmentionable" deserved to be shared. *But,* in the flow of an everyday life the soul's relevance wasn't obvious, for instance, at women's coffee's or at the office water cooler. The soul, mentioned in quieter, more focused moments of ordinary life, or dragged from the journals of the mystics for special occasions, was just there, part of our vocabulary, somewhere within our culture, a reference point that called us out of the mundane and stretched our imaginations to contemplate ...inside...outside...part of, attached to our bodies...whatever!"

Attending parochial school Liz was told by the nuns that each person has "a soul." They added, "God is very interested in your soul" and that was because "The soul was a place within each one of us that God kept special just for Himself." Nevertheless, mention and emphasis placed on the subject in everyday life outside of holy realms. Being a prayerful person, Liz noted the prayers of the saints oozed with soul yearning, and the Bible, "my soul thirsts," "my soul magnifies." Wow. That's powerful! Whatever it is.

Most Catholics were taught humans had souls but their pets and other creatures did not. Liz was ok with this. She decided the dogs, cats, birds and a myriad of creatures she befriended growing up didn't need souls. They were perfect the way they were. She could live with her conclusion and that was that the soul," though essential was kept for the afterlife. As she recalled, discussion was sort of placed on a "back burner" as to its relevance except, that is, to those who went to confession and, therefore, kept up a maintenance program for souls. This diligence was sort of like an insurance contract so that when we left our body behind on earth, the condition of our souls would eventually determine our admittance when arriving at "the Gate." At this time, Peter checked the records and made a determination of our levels of fitness for the Kingdom.

As far as Liz could understand, the soul was an intricate invisible part of human existence but always sort of ungraspable in simple communication or seemed to stall in attempting to go beyond with words. There seemed no words sufficient to give form to the profound.

And then one night Liz attended her friend, Jen's, gathering at her home and met a little girl. She met Michelle.

She was three years old. She sat on the floor in an adjourning room and Liz caught sight of her through the open door. She was caught up in what she observed from a distance. As other children moved freely and in constant motion around her playfully and with ease, the little girl sitting in the center of all this activity remained seated. "Chelle," the name by which Liz came to know her, sat serenely, strangely unmoved by her position among the exuberant movements of the others. Every once in a while she reached and pointed and one of the children would stop what he or she was doing and hand her a toy. As a mother of three rambunctious children under age five, this scenario playing out in view across the room was troubling.

Jen, the hostess, as if noticing her new friend's interest, called Liz over to introduce her to her daughter and friends. Looking up from her position on the rug below, the little girl smiled. "My name is Michelle," she announced. Looking deep into her blue eye, noticing her fragile form and delicate features, Liz was instantly beguiled.

In the next few years she and Chelle were to grow in their friendship, as also the bond that developed between Jen and Liz. And what continued to emerge from that initial fascination was Liz's understanding of an innate tenacity, resilience, and what seems a "foreknowing" of those who, by what we have come to judge as "normal" standards have somehow been "overlooked by blessings of health and beauty." We who feel ourselves fortunate to enjoy both stumble over appearances. Until, like Liz, we are led to discover someone's personal qualities through a chance meeting followed by personal invitation. To Liz, conscious choice to seek out the ill the vulnerable or disabled whose presence remained on the edges of our busy lives was the calling of certain gifted and skilled people.

Knowing this little girl broke through all those standards with which Liz measured health and beauty and even more importantly, a person's value. She observed, while we, those of us, gushed with words of concern or sympathy, and gave our usual respectful attention to "those less fortunate," meeting Chelle challenged Liz to pause on many occasions to reevaluate. "While we were sad or uncomfortable with her afflictions, her acceptance and graciousness acted to counter our inabilities to accept her condition." Jen shared these qualities in Chelle's person by relating that, in her sad or down days Chelle would remind her, "It will be okay, Mommy." Her quiet assurance acted as a deterrent to self-pity by refocusing us on trust. She lived with an invisible "wholeness" within herself that denied what we saw as her limitations and, in entering her brokenness with her, we allowed ourselves to discover beauty we never saw until we shared her life as it was, and not as we thought it should be.

Spinabifita children, Liz learned, do not have long lifespans. The night Chelle died Liz drove to Jen's home. Death, when it happens does not alleviate the pain, as Liz learned, even when death is anticipated. That moment of separation gives loss its full devastating impact and life becomes more precious with those with whom you share. Liz knew grief and the struggles put upon us to release the treasured people in our lives. Even so as she entered and began to walk the length of the hallway to Chelle's room the experience of releasing a child and the loss that was to follow was still just a dreading thought hanging heavy on her. Accompanying dread was premonition. Liz knew once she opened that door and entered Chelle's room she would have to deal with whatever experience awaited her and for which she knew she was not prepared.

Never in her wildest imaginings could she have anticipated the events playing out in those few moments that changed her forever. The fact that she did not close the door behind her evidenced the unfolding scene that stunned her immediately upon entering. The room was dark except for the light from Chelle's lamp by the bed. Jen was sitting on the edge of the bed holding her daughter who, after weeks of Jen's home nursing, lay limp and lifeless in her mother's arms.

This is when Liz felt it. The air in the room was moving! It was not air that you breathe. It was outside of her, moving around her, full and all embracing. Her senses felt surrounded by its movement, alive, warm, like a living organism or ...Presence! This is when she heard Jen's words. "Come in. Come here. Look! See how beautiful. See how beautiful she is."

Whenever Liz recalls this night she is forced to admit her inabilities to assimilate, to fathom, to take it all in. " It scared me out of my mind!" she told Jen later. As time passed and she had grasped some objectivity, she knew that this was as truthful a description, not only the experience, but also her reaction to what was out of the realm of anything she had ever known. She turned abruptly and left, closing the door softly behind her.

Years later when Jen and Liz shared that night Jen explained that throughout Chelle's last days she took on all the ravaging changes of her body as it deteriorated. "But," Jen explained, "in death she was transformed again into "my baby." She became soft and warm and pink and I wanted you to see." Of course, as time passed, they shared that most likely what Jen was experiencing that night was what is known as "an anointed moment" which was for Jen and Jen alone. And not what Liz would have seen if she had remained with her friend.

But then, Liz knew what she did experience that night was real. Its effects on her were real. She had in those three years of their friendship, received her own vision, awakened by this little girl who pointed inward to what was hidden and let it shine out to those of us who spent time with her. All through her life those moments of sadness, yearning, feelings awakened when Liz hardly expected them, were consistent and confusing... like full moon on the lake, the chamber orchestra playing Mozart, Bach, the Jazz and the Jesus of the blacks, their Blues, stories of Saints, simple love stories of Titanic proportions, folklores...all of which would make her pause...and there was Peggy Lee singing in her velvet voice, "Is this all there is?" Was it? Is It?

Up until the night Chelle died these were all these experiences fleeting, unshared, unimportant in the scheme of things. It was not so much the experience of an unknown, untouched reality that remained with her after that night as much as it was, and still is, what it awakened within her that turned her into a writer, a poet, a spiritual teacher, and, like Chelle, a person unafraid of what is unknowable and being brave to encounter what she has since learned to call her "Soul."

In ministry, occasionally someone would ask, "What is the soul?" Liz had learned that simplicity is the easiest avenue to pursue when struggling with complexity. Discovering most inquiries come from ordinary people seeking to understand spiritual realities, she began to use words that worked the best for her...and, she noted, "Jesus used for the sheep herders, the farmers, tax collectors, land owners... words that linked the spiritual with everyday reality." And though mystery will always invite and tease, most of us, Liz discovered, enjoy theology brought down to us in words we understand.

"What is the soul?" A little pondering and it would come to her. She always quoted the nun who told her that "your soul is that part of you that God claims for Himself alone."

Or, as she had come to a conclusion after knowing Chelle: "Our souls draw us out of our protected egos to struggle with the profound. And if we let our souls lead us, we will stay with those things we do not understand until each in its time becomes clear, real and redemptive."

Gradually, becoming more comfortable with her own "Soul" freed up her imagination: "When we sleep, and our minds and bodies are at rest, this is when our souls sneak out to converse with God." And, she would add, "get together with other souls...enjoy a social life that keep them alive in "the good Life" which they share with us upon return every morning while we are still only half awake and very receptive."

Liz knows the night Chelle died her soul wanted her to stay. "It was good for me to be there."

Before then she never gave her soul enough respect and attention and would hurry on to other things she had been taught were more important, more productive, sensible, safe. As she explained later, "I was frightened out of my mind!" Years later she reached the truth and this was "Evidently that is exactly where God wanted me...out of my mind... so the Spirit could touch my heart."

> "And delicate creatures
> gifted at birth
> will continue to haunt
> and beautify the earth.
> And all whom they touch,
> will love."

Chapter 12

As time grew closer to her visit to Minnesota, Liz found herself becoming distracted by a growing impatience Not only had it been a year since she had seen her children, there was also the years spanning between Jen her last time together. The word "ambivalent" returned to haunt her. She looked forward to her return to Minnesota, at the same time wondering at the impact of such a mass reunion.

Clare had made her weekly call to check if plans were moving along. As Liz ended the call and reached for her second cup of morning coffee, her mood began to darken. Jeremy came to mind and stayed in her thoughts all day. Why did New York have such a hold on her? Why was she still reluctant to return to the Midwest, which, by all sensible evaluations, she agreed with Clare, "is where you belong, Mom...with family and old friends."

Her reflections were suddenly interrupted by a voice in high pitch outside her windows. As she drew closer to look out, her attention moved to the gardens in front of the building. Before her search picked up the tiny figure below, it was the words and their pitch that drew her. "Mommy's here. Mommy's here!" came the words in a melodious chant. Once targeting a flurry of activity in the ground cover of the garden, a human form came into her view. A woman in an ankle length coat and a matching hat shielding her head against the winter chill, was moving back and forth, arms outstretched, chanting to what appeared to be birds landing and encircling her...pigeons!

They were landing, taking off, gliding back into this frenzied feeding ritual that plainly seemed to intensify with what she perceived was joyful anticipation. And all the while the woman repeated her high pitched chant. "Mommy's here. Mommy's here." Liz turned from the window surprised at the sudden delight that took hold of her. She found herself grateful for the shift from anxiety to amusement as her curiosity piqued. "What's this thing about pigeons?"

Just last week as she sat reading in the garden, a young man in what she would describe as a dapper hat and wearing, clearly what she noted, an expensive cashmere coat, looking as if he were on his way home after work, entered the circled clearing and began to empty his pockets of "tiny pellets" of feed. It took but a few seconds to entice pigeons out of the surrounding shrubs and vegetation. Liz forgot her book and let herself become engaged in what seemed to be a familiar interaction of city dwellers, human and critters. When he had exhausted the feed in his pockets he looked up, acknowledging her presence, and shook his head as if his actions pleased and puzzled simultaneously "I can't help it," he said to her. "I just love these little guys!" And, just as he appeared, he turned suddenly and walked behind the shrubs out of sight.

Evening was settling on Manhattan and its shadows were beginning to show through the blinds. Liz prepared food for supper and poured herself a glass of wine, relaxed into cushions and allowed herself to return to the theme playing out in her mind...pigeons. Pigeons lived in great numbers on and under the el train beams in the Bronx, right outside the entrance to Van Courtland Park where she grew up. On their walks with her father on Sunday afternoons, which began quite early in her life, when she was about three years old, her "daddy" taught her many things She ran through old overgrown wheat fields and enjoyed the rush of excitement as she flushed pheasants hiding in the wheat, overcame her fear of the "swamp creatures" to discover the beauty of all forms of life hidden there. Even today she remembers the fun of feeding the pigeons! Yes, because her father's way was to lure them to her hands! She would let him fill her palms with peanuts. When she was ready, she raised both palms, to face upward, fingers curled...and wait. In seconds the first pigeon would fly down and perch on her fingers. She would laugh as the others followed. There were too many to fit, so they would each grab a nut, fly away and others would take their place. Oh, the joy she would feel at their touch and the noise of their wings beating the air as each worked to balance for snack time.

Liz had saved many pictures of herself with her father during those early years. However, she didn't think back until the years past, on what may have been his pleasure as he shared her wonder and excitement. "He must have received great joy in watching me learn about the world he loved so much...the natural world." As she had aged she found herself wondering about others who shared her childhood. Or questioning what she may have missed in those early experiences. Jeremy came instantly to mind. What followed was a sadness and wondering if she were taking full advantage of their trips to New York, and not missing opportunity. "Perhaps this is why we return to our homes...not to assure ourselves that our memories are real, but perhaps, as with she and Jeremy, we are searching for, not only what we did not want to forget, but perhaps for those secrets locked away in the people who lived those memories with us What is it we may have missed in our youthful self-preoccupations? And if these contain a reality that awaits our curiosity. Does failure to explore and to question deny us the full measure of our life's experience?"

As their visits to New York continued, Jeremy surprised her with his decision to invest in an apartment with the intent of making plans to becoming a resident. By now their relationship had brought them closer, familiarity encouraging more discussion on their trips. She promised herself to delve deeper. To counter not only Jeremy's obvious reluctance to follow her beyond a certain point in conversation, but through a gentle persistence, she hoped to probe thosesudden shifts of Jeremy's moods she noticed

Of the four siblings, she and Jeremy had always been drawn together by, it seems, their similar perspectives. And then there was the humor that rose to the top of so many of their discussions. Even the most serious had a double edge that left each of them, with anticipation of their next meeting. To her, all of this boiled down to one word, "trust." Their lives forked out in different directions when, in her teens, the draft called her older brothers, Charles and Jeremy, into the service during the Second World War. Separated for two decades they had been given the opportunity later in years to take up where they left off. At the time of their father's death Charles was living in Florida, Jeremy in California, she in Minnesota and Tim, her youngest brother, serving in Vietnam…Death and funerals did not sit well with Liz in her younger years. Along with her insistence on keeping those dark times at a safe distance, she discovered as she stood over her father's coffin that evening at the mortuary in Fort Lauderdale, her aversion to "gathering around the body." It wasn't until she witnessed the grieving's reaction to the closings of the caskets before gathering for prayer, and was enlightened by an explanation of the need for some of us to experience the visual to reach closure, that she became resigned and, eventually, respectful. Now, as she gazed at her father's body. "He isn't here," she told herself. "Why is everyone gathered as if you are the host? And you aren't even here!" Emotionless, she turned and looked into Jeremy's silent stare from across the room. As if propelled by similar reactions, they walked towards one another She bent her head forward to hear his whisper, "Follow me." She followed him out into the humid air and down the street, knowing where he was going. They walked the four blocks to the beach in silence.

They continued to walk along the shore, neither seeming to want to mar the moment with talk. Jeremy was first to speak. "Dad wasn't there," Liz answered, "No. He is here." Their dad, the nature lover, the fisherman who waked at sunrise to fish in "the best hours for bass," who spent his summer weekends dressed in cut-off trousers, a lure bag draped on his shoulder, walking along the seashore. "It is called surf fishing," he explained. Their dad had skinny legs, which she was relieved, two of her brothers had inherited, and not she. Liz used to say, "He moved so quickly along the beach he looked like a sandpiper in trunks."

She and Jeremy walked as the sun set and breathed deep the evening air. They breathed as if each inhale, warm and humid- soft, was like a balm to their spirits. "As if dad's presence fills everything around us," Liz whispered. "His soul left the funeral home. He's here." They breathed him in like the salt in the air. That night would always be special to Liz.

Liz walked to the wall in the living room, and took Jeremy's picture from the shelf over the couch. Holding it, she let her gaze linger on his eyes, tender, sad, pondering eyes. That night of their father's funeral was the first time Liz could recall Jeremy expressing words of love and respect for their dad. Otherwise, she wasn't overly concerned nor did she ever question Jeremy's neutral stance when they discussed their dad. Unlike their mother. The fact that discussions about their mother brought on tart comments often puzzled Liz. What else was there to uncover from a person, your brother, whom you think you know after almost a lifetime together? Mention their dad and Jeremy became quiet and reminiscent. Mention their mother and her brother tensed and became irritated. Dare she ask?

Yes! She will ask all of those questions she never asked of the living when she had the chance. Being present at her parents' funerals, and that of her youngest brother brought the stark realization of the void in relationships by out failure to ask the important questions of the living at a time when they could have revealed so much. And possibly could have filled in the deep chasms that needn't have been.

Supper eaten and dishes put away, Liz walked into the bedroom and removed a locket from her jewelry case. Opened, the antique gold locket revealed a tiny photo. Liz had gifted her grandchildren with most of the family heirlooms as each child matured. However, this one she treasured and could neve willingly part with. Through the years she opened the tiny gold locket and studied the picture within. Since most of the picture was cut to fit this tiny piece of jewelry, it was difficult to distinguish any more then the face of a baby, chubby cheeks, eyes bright with innocence, smiling directly into the camera.

Liz knew her parents gave birth to a girl a year and a half before she was born. Rita was born in 1933, if she had figured correctly. As the Depression of 1929 was playing down, their family included Charles, Jeremy and Rita. The most Liz could ever draw from her parents when she questioned them about Rita was, "She was a chubby, blond, beautiful baby." And, most likely to accommodate her innocent curiosity, would add, "One evening she went into convulsions and died at the hospital the next day. We never found out what caused her convulsions." That was it. In her years of growing up Liz never heard mention of Rita from her parents or her brothers. Suspecting people of that time were never encouraged to express their grief other than door wreaths and black clothing, she accepted their guarded accounts. How she came to possess this gold locket Liz couldn't remember. Over the years she would hold it, gaze at the child in the photo and instinctively know it was Rita, and that her mother carried Rita around her neck and close to her heart in this tiny gold locket. "Did it strengthen her to carry her grief?"

What fueled the locket's significance for Liz and, remained to break in at certain times in her life, was the fact that at the time of Rita's death her mother was pregnant. Liz was born within months of her sister's passing. During a time of heavy introspection she was able to piece together the dynamics that she noticed between her mother and father as she grew up. For one thing, she and her mother did not have a closeness that Liz observed in other mother-daughter relationships. After time spent counseling, she concluded her being born into a family in grief left its mark on her with an ever present unexplainable feeling of separation ... abandonment. "My mother was in grief. When I was born she didn't have the emotional capacity to meet the needs of a newborn. So, in love, she went through the motions." Her dad, she began to suspect, overcompensated. He adored Liz. And, to make things worse, over the years, although he had three sons, he would playfully refer to her as "my favorite son." In spite of Liz and her mother lacking in their emotional connection, she never doubted her mother loved her. Silently transmitted from behind her mother's beautiful brown eyes was love expressed in the care she gave to each of her children. Accompanying the sadness that seemed to check its full expression was love shown in their mother's daily attention. She filled their dinner table every night with delicious meals, and their lives with order and a stability.

However, as Liz recollected, through her first few years, her mother's constant vigilance had to become stressful for the family. It became a mantra ... "Take the baby with you" or "Watch your sister," which meant "Don't run off," as young healthy boys do, but "stay with her in the yard." Fear of losing another child...fear of losing me "not only left its effects on me." Liz realized as she still pondered the family dynamics, "but drew in her brothers who, instead of a normal concern that grows with responsibility, plainly absorbed an irrational fear that stayed with them.

Liz allowed herself a laugh of sad irony. "My poor brothers. They were still hovering over me in my teens. They took turns checking me when I got sick on New Year's Eve. Charles, plainly educated by the curiosity of his peers, had shared with Jeremy that I might be "getting my monthly period for the first time. Since mom and dad are out with friends, we will check in on her," he instructed his younger brother. Their pact which Jeremy described years later was so touching Liz fought the pull to be diverted by the humor. "I don't even remember why I was sick that night. But I do remember wondering why you and Charles were poking your heads in the bedroom door on a night I knew you were out with friends."

Her youngest brother, Tim, survived the Vietnam War only to be brought down by the hepatitis virus at the young age of forty six. She followed behind the caissons at Arlington Cemetery on a cold dreary day right before Christmas Eve. Her whole being dragged forward to the steady beat of the drums marking each step along the route to the gravesite. Charles, her oldest brother's gasping sounds startled Liz. She reached forward and touched him on the shoulder, She asked, "Are you alright?" aware through her own tears that this was the first time she had witnessed her oldest brother break. It seemed as if his tears engulfed him beyond his attempts to hold them. The sudden force seemed to send currents through his body. She kept in step but her eyes never left her brother's agony as he fought against the stark reality of losing his "baby brother."

Oldest child's stance against weakness. After all, the family depends on him. Liz understood how her oldest brother even often played the role of "stand in" for one or the other parent. More than a few times, Charles came to the rescue. Today, she wanted to come to his rescue.

Grief can bury the living, too. Through her ministry training Liz learned the tragedy of our refusal to take time out to listen to what grief teaches. Guarding the secrets behind our emotions stifles not only the person carrying the grief, but plants a wedge of fear between them and life. This senseless waste of a person's energy and potential in being over responsible, keeping our emotions tamed and unattended until they gush during times of loss makes living fully and alive unattainable. On that trip to Washington, D.C., Liz's resolved to renegotiate a different course for her family's future. Charles took it all on and as the years brought more and more responsibilities, and the pressures of being the oldest and first born son grew, so did his addictions. He referred to Liz as "our perennial child." Poor Charles, so responsible. Poor me," Liz lamented. "I was in my forties when I finally discovered the pain and the thrill of maturity."

Liz glanced at the clock on her dresser. An hour had passed and she was still gazing at the face of the child in the locket, letting her mind wander unchecked. Recalling the trip home from Washington and Tim's funeral had presented a major turning point for her. It was on her return to Minnesota that year that she planned her strategy. And now she had to follow through. Jeremy was going to relate his account of Rita's death. What happened that evening? And where was her precious brother the day his little sister died? She knew now that it was these events that made New York such a pivotal place to resurrect and renegotiate life. Her life. Jeremy's life. And her children's future perhaps. When the last ghost, left to pine on the East Coast, was finally laid to rest, maybe then she would be ready to call Minnesota her home.

Chapter 13

On September 11, 2001, Liz left the house early. She recalled her first day back to work after a family vacation in New York. That date, begun so ordinary and plunged into infamy as the hours passed and the events of the day grew to unbelievable proportions. Those first early moments, though, were still preserved in Liz's memory for the feelings of wellbeing just minutes away from her fall into a "black hole of despair," she would explain later.

She opened the door of her little Cooper and threw her purse in and, after adjusting windows and mirrors, turned the key and listened as her car groaned awake after a long nap. "Wake up, lazy bones," she quipped. Time to get back to the real world." Liz had just returned from two weeks in New York and felt herself almost buoyant with anticipation. She was actually looking forward to starting the new season at St. Joseph's. Retreating into the Manhattan scene with Jeremy and, this time, joined by two of her children and their spouses, proved a four- star on the vacation charts. Being able to experience her favorite city through the fresh excitement and fascination of youth, and observing Jeremy's playing the doting uncle, created a world of playful spontaneity with her precious brother at the helm.

Liz was relaxed as she drove slowly to the church, "Jeremy and I were reliving familiar scenes through the children's eyes." Her pleasure returned remembering their sense of adventure and anticipation showing clearly on their faces each morning. Each day they experienced for the first time the sights and sounds, the diversity and stately structures of history offered by the city people called "the center of the world." Liz grew up enjoying fashion, music, theatre, literature and the stock reports fresh in the world news before they were filtered through communications to the rest of the world. Added to her joy was the interest of the four "tourists" as she and Jeremy embellished their daily ventures with personal stories.

On the first morning, Jeremy had surprised everyone with their very own "fun card." He looked like "the teacher" standing in front of them lined up to receive instructions. With an upward glance and a roll of his eyes that communicated, "you're gonna love this!" he presented Metro Cards, passes for rides on all buses and subways in Manhattan, as if he were presenting merit awards to outstanding students. Thus, the years were never able to darken the significance of this trip in August of 2001. They spent one afternoon touring The Stock Exchange, the Native American museum both of which precluded a ferry ride to Staten Island. They had just launched and when a scene from her past made her chuckle

Prom night for Aquinas High closed with a ride on the Staten Island Ferry. "Prom night! Oh, the pain of recall," she sighed. How uncomfortable adolescence, especially dates coerced, as hers was, in those last frantic weeks. Every year there are those, like Liz, who find themselves approaching the social event of high school year dateless! However, even worse than that, Liz learned, was to find herself on the Staten Island Ferry on a summer night, full moon, warm breeze, dressed in a knock-out lace and silk creation that took agonizing weeks to find, only to discover the boy next to her on whom she was placing her expectations of her most romantic fantasies, was a complete stranger! Oh, he looked good...great, for that matter. But the problem emerged when she realized the ingredients of friendship and common interests got lost in the planning. "Parents of the young man were probably at home that evening sorting through the receipts from their son's frenzied search for a suit, shirt, tie, flowers, tickets, and God knows what he went through to be on that boat next to this girl whom he passed in the hallways, the recipient of a sparse few mumbled sentences over a crowded lunch table and whose closeness now made him dizzy, causing his tongue to jam as the fragrance from her perfume sent him into a panic."

Jeremy's voice rose from beside her as they stood along the deck railing amidst the murmurings of those sharing the space around them. She resisted his charms and returned to her thoughts. "Wouldn't it be fun to set aside some time at a party to coax men to tell prom stories?" she mused. This might even make hilarious dinner conversation tonight." On reconsideration, she added, "And it could turn out disastrous! Forget that idea!"

During breakfast at the Comfort Diner the next morning her brother rolled out his itinerary list and announced to us that we would be boarding the train to Woodlawn station, the last stop on the Bronx line. From hindsight, she was sure Jeremy had no premonition as to what awaited them when they emerged from their first ride on an el train to the Bronx. At that early stage of their trek, an obvious motive seemed to be to introduce the children to where we grew up. Later, Liz wondered, if in the later planning stage, her brother became aware of a deeper motive and, thus, our stop at "Jeremy's Rock." Whatever the case, Liz suspected the group experience was more than any of them anticipated.

In a wooded clearing in Van Cortland Park where the Bronx and Yonkers meet there is a rock, a huge rock...a humungous, gargantuan, solid boulderish rock! Black... and, for a three year old boy, as high as the eye can see! This we referred to as "Jeremy's Rock." It still reigns over the space today like a giant whale.

The "Whale" was set among the trees about half a mile down from the walking paths. Jeremy and Liz stood, her eyes followed the movement of children on the surface of the rock. Looking in the direction of Jeremy's concentration, Liz saw it, too, was drawn to the figures playing on the Rock. It was clear to see that boys outnumbered the girls. Boys of all sizes climbed over and down its sides and across the top of the solid silent giant. No doubt its hulk took on the sculpting of decades of multiple foot sizes and jean slicks. Weather-beaten, its body was ribbed for climbing by generations of storms. Jeremy's voice interrupted her imaginings.

"I didn't anticipate how much I am enjoying seeing it again." He paused and Liz waited.

"I've been standing here contemplating and have decided for some mysterious reason I can't recall, I felt very happy in this place. Happy maybe as in "free." I'm feeling really good right now. And watching those little guys scaling the heights as I used to, ...well, it appears as though their play is responsible for my present good feelings. It's almost as if I am being transported through them to a place somewhere inside of me that I feel forced to remember....no...not forced...invited. Invited is the word."

She turned to look at him and saw the familiar frown and intensity in his eyes as he perused the horizon or the furthest distance of a room as if this strategy provided space to organize his thoughts. These moments were always preludes to provocative discussions over the dinner table; and at other times, some were held for lighter moments, such as tidbits of humor between guitar renderings with occasional sips from a bottle of Heinekens No matter, substitute red wine for the beer and Liz had no doubts as to how much alike they were.. She watched as he walked away from her to join one of the boys on the rock. Whatever Jeremy asked, the boy moved closer and joined in conversation. Her attention gradually left Jeremy and led her to look for the "four tourists," the title chosen for them over coffee that morning. The others seemed thoroughly entranced studying the phenomena before them, and after a thorough touch test of the Rock's surface, including the lower ridges for seating comfort, had wandered down a path into the woods.

• • •

Very subtle, at first, and then her hearing became attuned to the gentler sounds, children laughing, birds songs, the drone of insects, and, as the sun grew higher she grew warm. She lifted her head to feel the heat of its rays on her face and closed her eyes. Jeremy's Rock loomed majestically against her inner vision... "like a mountain, or a giant redwood...solid, grounded in time, dependable in change. What has added to the joy of this day is the assurance gained from witnessing this magnificent piece of nature that is still giving life to the children through each generation." To listen to Jeremy as he struggles with the discovery of the little boy who still lives inside of him. She turned to find Jeremy and noticed he was alone, sitting with his back resting against the tree trunk ...looking contented, as if his mind brought him someplace and he didn't want to be disturbed. The sun casts shadows on him, the leaves moved in the breeze. Jeremy sat covered in leaf shadows."

As the afternoon waned behind clouds they gathered for departure. Liz turned to draw in the scene one last time and noticed each of the others was drawn to look back as they began their exit from the clearing. Sometimes you don't have to be told. You just know you have stood for a while on holy ground.

"The President and his family left the White House moments ago for an undisclosed destination." The voice on the radio cut through Liz's thoughts with a strange urgency. She pulled into the parking lot and sat trying to understand the words that were being transmitted from the car radio. The voice was alarming and his speech rapid. Her heart accelerated. She felt fear rising and her thoughts struggling to make sense out of what she was hearing. She heard the seat belt hit against the window but didn't lessen her speed except to slam the door behind her. Her breathing rang in her ears as she ran across the parking lot and entered the church. When she reached the front lobby, Nancy was not at her post. The reception room and lobby was empty. She heard the gasps, her breathing heavy with fear as she hurried down the hall and thrust herself through the first open door. Nancy was leaning intensely forward, Fr. Paul sat rigid, Anne beside him, the postal man with a package still balanced on his lap. Their eyes looked forward and fixed on the TV screen.

A plane had rammed into one of the Twin Towers in downtown New York City! Moments later another plane was caught by the camera bursting into flames as it slammed into the other tower and exploded. Moments went by, each scene folding into another, like a stack of motion cards. And black, like dark flecks, began appearing like birds flushed from their cover, airborne. That is when she heard Anne gasp,

"My God, those are people jumping from the windows." They were jumping out of windows to escape the flames! Seconds later, Tower One went into a slow "bow" and began to lean forward. At first it bent like its neck was top-heavy. What followed was a scene in motion that those watching will never forget. The building came down in a gradual melt as those once magnificent arches that braced the structure, bent grotesquely like steel under a welder's torch A curtain of thick smoke filled the air and, like grey gauze, pulverized debris descended over the view in a shade of death that extinguished all life forms on the ground below. Anything and anyone moving after that took on a ghostly appearance. Moving and rising from the streets below were people, hundreds of people struggling for balance, covered with layers of descending ash.

The camera's panned for a moment for a shot of the skyline of lower Manhattan. Liz gazed transfixed, unbelieving. As the other second tower came down it had left a gaping space which, from a distance, showed New York City with a giant wound that burned for days and left the world waiting for life to bleed out, knowing it was just the beginning of an unbearable grief. Liz explained later, "I felt suddenly violated. It was perhaps the way a person feels when their homeland is invaded and soldiers forcibly enter their houses. The pain was deep in my belly, like the clutch before miscarriage. Perhaps it compared with the feeling I would have if someone shot my parents as I watched." Life, full of vigor and promise was ended and, according to the papers that week, they numbered more than three thousand men, women, babies, and the unborn.

Nothing much got done the day the Twin Towers came down...in St. Paul or anywhere else in the country. Liz sat at her desk and just stared blankly at the walls. Every now and then she could hear people returning and leaving the staff room. She, too, kept the vigil as reports kept describing events which deepened the wound as each moment intensified the horror unfolding.

The following week, with the world and America still reeling from what is now called "The 9/11 terrorist attack." Liz sorted through the photos of her family's visit to New York . One that stood out and one she cherishes is of her children standing on a balcony in Brooklyn, with the New York skyline making a proud backdrop. They are smiling, happy, having fun...and across the river two Towers cut the clear, blue morning skies above Manhattan ... just as they had the September morning three weeks ago that had begun with so much promise.

As the days passed Liz did what she had always done to express the sacred memorials of her faith. She took a photo of the Twin Towers, taken on one of her visits with Jeremy, and had it enlarged. With drapes, candles and symbols she created a prayer table in the lobby of St. Joseph's. She created a sacred space. She could bring her grief here. And, although her ties to New York remained in her deep and painful, she knew others needed comfort as well, and to be reminded once again of continuum, of hope that always accompanies us as we are led to the other side of tragedy.

Rage! It hit like a train...whoosh! What to do? Liz had been working at her desk when it engulfed her. "It had no explanation, no remedy, it just came on and stayed." A week later, exhausted from forcing composure and attempts at intellectualizing herself into moral behavior, Liz picked up the phone, "Paul, are you busy?"

When she entered Father Paul's office his gaze met hers immediately as if he had zeroed in on the doorway as soon as he hung up the phone. She met his gaze with a defiance that startled her. "Why?" she asked, And held up the morning newspaper. All week the local paper has announced details of the killing of a woman employed at the market a few blocks from the church. It was the initial report that came that morning a week ago, she realized in that instant, that triggered this rage. As the week went on, plans were being made to have a unified march of the three churches in the area to unite against violence. Liz had been notified and the ministers of the Lutheran and the Episcopal Churches were still waiting to hear from her.

"And have you responded?" Paul asked as if he were planning his move before an assault. Instead Liz became very calm and looked away. "I don't want to plan the march." When she focused again she saw the worried tilt of the priests head to one side as he worded his next question. "Liz, what is going on? Tell me."

And she did, the fury was out of the cage. "I am so angry! More than angry! I am appalled, I am furious, I am..." With eyes wide and paused to continue, Liz rose up from her chair and started to pace. "I don't want to be a part of this world that is turning on us. Why do the good die and evil keeps multiplying. I was so happy last month. So full of stories and good things to share, so grateful, thankful...Nuts! Bull! I am so angry that our country, and my city was violated...and this!" She picked up the newspaper and slammed it down onto the floor.

....a mother can't even feel safe on her job because some maniac or demented, confused, despicable animal thinks he's justified in gunning her down!

With clenched fists she hit his desk and the sound frightened and embarrassed her.

"Oh, God, I'm sorry...so sorry," she heard herself say. The walls spun as she gazed from side to side, dazed from the force of her unchecked outburst.

"I don't want to be a part of this world anymore. It is too cruel...the pain too relentless...too..." Liz looked for the nearest seat and slid back into it. Exhaustion claimed her like a giant wave gripping her and then taking her down.

Movement and sound was stilled as if waiting for a cue that never came.

"In this world you will have many troubles, but do not fear. I have conquered the world."

Father Paul was reading from the gospel of John! Suddenly her thoughts became fixed as if the words themselves drew her out. She starting to breathe again. A lightness, like fresh air, wafted in and filled her head.

The priest's quiet question broke through, soft and cautious in its inquiry.

"Are you still with us?"

Liz felt strange, like the effort to follow the sound strained her will to respond.

"Just barely," emerged her whisper.

She fought the urge to resist but the sound of his soft inquiry encouraged her forward. She lifted her head and focused her gaze to meet his. He was smiling!

He paused like a camper checking the terrain after a landslide, and then ventured further. She accepted the glass of water he offered. That is when she realized she had no clue to the unfurling of the next moment. Should she strive for some explanation to justify herself or just excuse herself and slink out of the room? Gratitude came easily when he took the lead,

"What are you going to do about the march?"

"I'm going to organize our parish to march with the other churches."

"Why?"

"Why? To show solidarity with the family and friends of the clerk, and with the people in this community, and ..."

She felt the tears welling up, along with a puzzling thrust of determination to stand against the evil that almost brought her to violence.

"And," she repeated, to stand with New York and maybe, just maybe, discover my own courage again by being a part of theirs. I know after today that I cannot face fear alone." She wasn't able to stop the flow of words. Perhaps her previous abandonment of discretion gave her confidence to trust that both of them would survive her restoration to sanity.

"I want to confess being absolutely terrorizing this week...and the language coming out of me could have curled wallpaper! After this week and my grand explosion, I am scary! What scares me even more as age closes in on me, is that I may become one of those ladies...you know...the one in Memory Care rolling down the hallways in her wheel chair shouting profanities!"

Seemingly unfazed, Father Paul's parting comment then, as strange it was, remains an even stranger consolation for Liz in her present struggles with age and grace.

"So?" the priest answered, "It happens all the time."

Chapter 14

Dreams, like spirits that
move me on to journey
with those I meet.
Some stir and taunt me
still undaunt me
as I sleep.

Liz was startled awake by the thud of a delivery truck lowering its ramp onto the pavement below. It took a few blinks to adjust to her surroundings. She had taken off the week after Easter to spend time in New York with her brother. Arriving the night before at Jeremy's apartment she would await his arrival later that afternoon.

It had been almost six months since the attack on the Twin Towers. They had spoken on the phone and both were in agreement on their need to enter recovery with the people of New York. As the months had passed each of them discovered reasons very personal that intensified as they shared itineraries and made plans. Viewing the devastation on the TV screen, they agreed, hardly sufficed for the depth of experience necessary to expunge the pain of reality.

Thus, so many things only imagined became real as she and Jeremy approached the site the next day. The cavernous hole exposed the expansive size, the height and depth that once accommodated two magnificent structures that had loomed majestically over the Manhattan skyline. The work of so many visionaries who created two buildings perfectly balanced and fortified to stand as a permanent expression of the excellence and spiritual resilience of a city united against the forces of tyranny for over 200 years. Pulverized! Vanished! Now only a gravesite. In their place steel nets draped buildings that stood on the perimeters, like mourners in black. Chain-linked fences separated the cranes and diggers from the lines of public viewers. Liz followed Jeremy as they joined the viewers along the fence. Orange dividers marked the areas hundreds of feet below them. The markers defined the dig like road warnings the length of city blocks! Jeremy's reaction matched her thoughts. "My God...how could anything that magnificent just disappear!"

"Hundreds of people looking on, tourists for the most part. This, only a presumption, as the faces of everyone wore the same grim sadness and disbelief, following, mutely, or whispering to one another in stunned reverence. Their somber tones filtering through the distant sounds of drills and pounding, like mourners waiting for a voice to cut in and add some sense to all of this. Until then, stark reality seemed to nudge its way in with each step along the lines, creating a slow path into the American psyche. What seemed a diabolic act to a civilized western mind had no comparisons in the American consciousness, no precedence from which to articulate. For this reason even time may not provide sufficient answers for all the unspoken questions of those who mourned with us that day."

"Liz! Look! Can you believe...!" Jeremy's voice cut out as he stared in amazement. St. Paul's, the little church across the street from the site, stood like a brave elder amidst the surrounding excavation seemingly untouched and serene against the unfolding trauma and its invasive sounds. There were plaques along the path in the court outside the church, one of which caught Jeremy's attention. He stopped to read a plaque by what appeared to be a large tree trunk. He looked up and waited for Liz to join him." The tree was credited for intercepting the full impact of 9/11, saving the church from impact and flying debris." Up close they could see the base of its trunk had been preserved to stand as a memorial among the grave stones in the church yard. Moving on, they walked through the graves and noticed the dates on the stones, some dating back to the 1700's. Jeremy halted and returned to the memorial Tree.

Liz, who had been following behind paused and stared at the name over the church entrance. She blinked and continued to search her memory... "London during the Second World War! Yes! Yes!" she repeated and quickened her pace to catch up to Jeremy. Her hand reached out to rest on Jeremy's shoulder. "St. Paul! St. Paul's Cathedral! She watched as his face lit with understanding. "The Blitz!"

"Yes, the Blitz that destroyed everything around the Cathedral in London except..." Her sentence was halted by her brother's amazed response. "Except the Cathedral of St. Paul!" he completed her sentence. "That's an amazing connection, little sister." It always amused her to notice that quizzical half grin and a gentle repetitive nod of affirmation with which Jeremy received fresh insights, as if the up and down cranial motion registered information for further reflection.

They entered the church quietly. St. Paul's was a little church and so, its main room revealed its recent past in full view from the entry. Filling its large worship space, where the rescuers and wounded sought refuge those first weeks, there were walls of memorabilia, pictures, banners, letters, notes, uniforms, hard hats, flags, videos. Liz and Jeremy began to realize as they exchanged comments, that even the massive presentation of photos and on-sight videos., as good as they were, fell short in portraying the personal experience of actually being present in Manhattan on September eleventh two thousand one. With that considered, the impact was, none the less, soul shattering. This day lingered with her as Liz attempted to describe their experience to others, knowing she could only gather the fragments, the leftovers pieced together by the victims' accounts through visual presentation. " Pausing to step into history; to leave ourselves open to absorb the spiritual embodiment of human suffering presented in that room at St. Paul's, piqued my senses," Liz would describe, 'in the most extraordinary way. For a moment, as horrific the scenes, I found myself wishing to have been there on that day. Strange as it was, from the moment of entry, and following the images around the room, I was filled ... awed...humbled!" The courage and sacrifice freely poured out from the responders in the aftermath filled her consciousness and grew and filled and became a presence around her. She felt herself lifted with the images of those who walked, ran and drove into hell, and then felt herself descend with them in the space where she stood. She would always remember feeling empty and sad beyond words. "It was like I had moved inside a pulsing wound that was alive and hovering heavy, like a dirge, in the air," she would try to explain. Liz knew, even being present to experience what was preserved from the first terrorizing hours and weeks, she would never be qualified to adequately communicate the bravery and compassion portrayed by the displays that lined the church walls. She also knew that, somehow, by standing on that site, surely made holy by the spilling of innocent blood, she and Jeremy and those thousands of daily visitors experienced an unexplainable transformation that would change them forever.

Jeremy suggested a brisk walk after they emerged from the church. They walked until Liz tired and called time out. "Whew, let's slow down. I feel like I did when I was trying to keep up with dad. He could outwalk me when he was seventy. And I was in my thirties then. Now I'm older and you're wearing me out!" They rounded the gate at Bowling Green and stopped to catch a breath before continuing. "There it is!" Liz pointed as they came to Wall Street. Jeremy, in the lead as usual, braked himself. "There what is?" "The New York Stock Exchange." Liz didn't wait for Jeremy's response. "...where our dad worked for thirty years! Jeremy slowed and joined her "to pay homage to the family landmark" he explained. Liz stood taking in the building, the flag, the cobblestoned streets. "Daddy took me here when I was twelve years old. We stood on the balcony and watched people running in all directions...like ants." Noting Jeremy's impatience, she moved ahead down the street until a beautiful old building loomed into sight...the Francis Tavern on Pearl Street!

Entering, they were transported by the tavern's interior "old, solid, spacious and elegant". Liz peered from the lobby around to the front room with its cozy style of the 1700's and warmed to the atmosphere instantly. The host guided them through the halls into a series of rooms of various sizes and decor,

"It's sort of like being greeted by an old friend," Liz commented.

"Or the ghost of Marley but, for sure, old, very old" Jeremy interjected.

Jeremy's grunt assured her of his lack of enthusiasm for antiquity or, she hesitated, "maybe he is reserving comment until he checks the tap room.

"Should I be interested in a pot pie that George Washington considered delicious back in the 1700's?" Jeremy was perusing the menu. "It sounds suspect...hmm...old...musty...not very appetizing after all this time."

"And should you be making fun of dead heroes?

"Ahh...now you're talking." His expression lightened as the Heineken's was set on the table in front of him. Liz sipped her brandy on ice and waited. They had been led to a booth nestled quietly in a corner. She felt the tensions of the day ease and feelings of overwhelming affection rise as she settled her gaze on this slender, handsome man across the table from her. She knew there wasn't anyone she would rather be with. The realization brought her contentment.

"I'm sorry. This is not a time to be making jokes about heroes." Jeremy's tone had softened. Liz stared at his contrite expression and couldn't help smiling when she noticed his silverware lined neatly on the napkin in front of him.

As if noticing Liz's amused expression he added, "I travel a lot and sometimes eating establishments look pretty grungy. The best assurance of cleanliness is to check the table setting and determine if the condiment containers have been wiped clean. So, if you're wondering, I got in the habit of making sure the silverware is clean...down to the prongs on the fork. Then I check the carpet...make sure last night's crumbs aren't still strewn about, and..."

"And, dear brother, here I thought it was another of your eccentricities revealing itself."

"Nooo, my child," he corrected with a tone of mild indignation. And, with a roll of his eyes to accentuate his next comment. Anticipating her laughter, he continued, "You misjudge me. The fact that you overlook my outstanding qualities and irreproachable social behavior offends me deeply."

"And," Liz interrupted, "have you forgotten that I witnessed the pranks and light drama of our earlier years. One incident comes immediately to mind...Miami Beach... after the Frank Sinatra show. Now, close your eyes," she instructed, "I want you envision Collins Avenue in front of the Fontainebleau Hotel." Jeremy quickly assumed his role, and sat with eyes shut, rubbing his temples, even emphasizing the relevance of the moment with a gentle "Ummm." "Sush!" she reprimanded. "Alright, are you on Collins Avenue?"

"Yes. Yes. I'm there. I just emerged from the hotel and...I am holding something in my hand. Why, it looks like...it IS...a tablecloth!"

"Good!" Now notice the crowd merging onto the street below. Catch the movement in the crowd...got it...there is a figure who steps out to hail a taxi...in a white drape ...ah... Who is this draped figure? Yes, I see now. It is...oh, my goodness...my brother! There stands J. Gerard McKenna, hailing a taxi looking like Gandhi in an oversized diaper and tennis shoes! Ta da! I rest my case."

Jeremy stifled a smile and looked into the space above her. "Ah, yes. That was one of my best performances."

Jeremy was often amused and frequently amusing. But seldom was he prone to collapsing in loud, belly rippling laughter. Liz was the first to feel the server's presence at the table. "We apologize," she told the waiter between gasps as he served their fish and chips.

It was still early afternoon. They were relaxed and full, agreeing the fish and chips was a better choice than the lure of history. And delving into American history made as good a backdrop to her next move as she contemplated how to begin. She took the locket from her purse and placed it on the table. She sipped her Latte and chose her question, hoping it would present a gentle detour from American history and in the direction of their family history. "Jeremy," she begun, noticing her silence had already communicated the shift to Jeremy. Her brother leaned forward eyeing the small box she had placed in front of her. "Here," she urged as she moved it towards him, "open it."

Jeremy's movements were slow as he gently opened the box and brought out the locket.

"Where did this come from?"

"After mother died I discovered the locket among her jewelry. Ever since, this tiny locket with a baby's picture inside has intrigued me." She watched his expression as his interest grew. I have studied the photo often, and with the same interest. It's a photo of a child... a very young child. Who is it? And why was this picture stored among our mother's treasured keepsakes?"

"Rita...Rita, our sister?" Jeremy leaned backwards against the chair and pushed himself a few inches from the table, beer in hand. From that posture he appeared to be studying the spots on the ceiling. Liz felt her breath catch and hold as she waited.

"Wow, Rita! I haven't thought of her in decades. I was five and to me it seemed she was here and then gone. I mean "gone", like gone from the house, gone from mention, gone, gone! After a while it was like she never existed!"

"That's why I'm bringing her back...because she did exist and she isn't gone!"

The silence that followed was a welcomed pause in their efforts to process Rita's sudden emergence from years of shrouded silence imposed upon her.

"Rita's death has left a deep wound," Liz began in whispered tone, "that left our family numb. I know my mother didn't hold me, sooth me, and make me feel welcomed. I don't think Mom had the emotional capacity to feel anything and so she went through the motions. I was born into a family of grief! Our sister's sudden death affected our relationships, our family dynamics, and I know how she impacted my perspectives on life. That's because I had to give a talk on "Perspectives" and research led me right to Rita. I may not have been born yet, but I was holed up in mother's womb feeling and hearing the events on the other side of "the wall." Science has proven the baby receives sounds, emotions, and even trauma through the umbilical cord. You may not have recognized me, but I was there when Rita became ill and died. This is why I am asking you about my sister whose death still disturbs me. You, precious brother, are my last key to putting her at rest...for both of us, may I add."

Jeremy stood up. "Enough for today." He never figured the check sitting down. He would always push himself away from the table, reach for his wallet, bring the check up to eye level and, returning it to the table, stand like a teacher over his notes, peel each unfolded bill slowly, laying them neatly on the bill before turning to leave. Liz never knew why these little observations were so important to her. Time would bring them back to memory over the years and make her grateful.

"Give me some time to think. And then we will talk about this again." Jeremy was right. The day had overloaded their interest, and the demands initiated by her delvings promised to be a lengthier prospect worthy of dedication. It was time to leave those stirrings for another day.

Chapter 15

Stay with It
We'll do this together.
With the way life goes,
who knows?
We may discover
if we try,
A change of perception,
in either direction, and so..
here we go...are you ready?
Hold onto my hand.
Let's fly!

The dazzling complexity of hues created by brick and concrete, glass and metal, casts ever-changing reflections, like cubic art, onto city streets as the sun makes its daily pass over Manhattan This subtle light display has never ceased to captivate Liz. It stirs memories of her early years working in midtown when she completed her errands early in the morning. How magical the city seemed, especially on those days when the air was fresh and the sun was just tilting over the tops of the skyline. Her routes usually led her passed a garden oasis between buildings where people sat with their morning coffee under trees and canopies that had been strategically placed, no doubt, by city planners. To her, every morning was like "watching the curtain go up on live theatre," she reflected. "Every day fresh and spontaneous!"

"It seems so long ago." Liz sat looking out of the window of the Manhattan Diner. And then rephrased her comment, "It was long ago! Over fifty years long. That's long." Her statement was followed by pleasure to realize that she still drew delight from the city's landscapes, as well as the energy that emanated daily from the lure of the unpredictable. She sighed. "And speaking of the unpredictable, where is Jeremy?" They had planned to meet at the Diner after he decided to return to Central Park to "check out one of the vendors." Liz and Jeremy shared a mutual enjoyment of shopping. However, shopping with Jeremy, begun as a venture of pleasure, slowly transformed as hours passed, into a burden of a tedious research. This because Jeremy shopped with the same finesse that drove his dining habits. She winced as she recalled their treks through the men's department of several stores. After hours of growing futility to find just the right man's shirt, which had to have "two pockets," one for his notes and the other for his reading glasses of course! As their day wore on it became obvious that today's market did not manufacture many two-pocket shirts. Any sane person, she concluded, would eventually succumb to the inevitable. As the hours droned on she began to notice a change in her brother. His mood lifted and, to her horror, she discovered, he was enjoying the challenge. Unfortunately, by this time, she had lost interest, and was fighting off a growing irritation that began earlier in the hunt. Time and energy depletion later, nerves shredding, patience spent, she found herself diving for the nearest foxhole for shelter from the pain. Which, this afternoon, happened to be the Manhattan Diner on west 77th Street.

It was then that she noticed Jeremy standing on the street outside, wearing that familiar frown as he studied the exterior of the building. "It's one of my favorite eating spots," she assured him as he approached her table. "Comes with a guarantee you'll love it," she added.

"I didn't realize it was so far," he countered.

"I suppose you walked."

"All twelve blocks...good exercise."

"Don't tell me...you found one person in Manhattan who shares your passion for two-pocket shirts."

He settled in his seat and tried to look astonished, "How did you know?"

Liz waited for the punch line. Jeremy always drew one from his endless source of rye humor which, then, was followed by pretense of how astonished he was with the other person's perception. When he had sufficiently set the tone, he would time his explanation that made total sense...to him.

"Are you ready for this?" he began, "Remember that guy with the gold screwdrivers on keychains?"

Liz waited as he ordered his Heineken. And, when he was sure her irritation was sufficiently diverted and his wanderings justified, he continued. "I bought you a gift."

Upon inspection Liz noticed each set of two tiny gold screw drivers were a different size at each end and sported the meticulous addition of screw tops to insure they stayed intact on your keychain or in a purse. "Amazing! They're so unique!"

"I bought several...for gifts." He sipped and continued to look pleased that he had won her over.

As they ate Jeremy quieted. Liz suspected it was fatigue. She was wrong. His words began slowly.

"Now, about Rita. Since you brought it up I've really been thinking trying to recollect the night she died." This announcement was followed by a long pause and, it appeared, a check of her posture on the other side of the table before he continued. Noting she had moved into the table with an instant curiosity, he bent forward and looked into her eyes. "I lived it but don't let your expectations rely on my immediate answers to your questions." His eyes turned sad and vulnerable. "That look," Liz thought. Familiar because it is in his photos. The look that reaches out seeking gentle engagement."

"I was alone with Rita the evening she got sick, that is, until I recalled dad dozing on the couch in the living room."

"So, not really alone. Daddy was there. Where was Mother?"

Jeremy ordered coffee for them and she waited as he gathered his thoughts and continued.

"I asked myself the same question. I know for sure she wasn't there. Neither was Charles. Sometimes on errands he'd help her carry packages or groceries.

He cupped his chin in one hand and leaned his elbow onto the table and sighed. Liz waited. "What I'm trying to say is, it was a normal day, nothing amiss or unusual," he explained, at the same time, sounding impatient with his inability to capture evasive details. This said, Jeremy seemed to withdraw from the conversation. Liz sipped her coffee and watched as his attention gradually returned.

"Hey! This is like raising the dead! It's agony! I was only five." He added cream and stirred his coffee slowly.

"After hours of probing and pondering the slumbering past, it came to me why my memory picked up that I was alone with Rita. Dad fell asleep!"

"Dad fell asleep?"

"Well, yes. You know how he used to come home and then fall asleep after dinner."

"Every night almost, maybe twenty minutes or half-hour...his "power nap."

"Are you telling me it is that simple...our dad fell asleep?"

"Why not?" It was an ordinary day in the life of a normal family. When Liz didn't respond, he continued.

"Rita was crying." I remember taking her out of the crib. I still have memory of what plastic baby pants feel like. She must have come over the railing fanny first and against my cheek as she tumbled She stopped crying! I can only imagine how that went over to a five year old. I solved the immediate problem."

Something flashed into Liz's mind. "I am smiling because I remember how you used to entertain me. You brought your own characters into my doll house. When I think back to Detective Charlie Chan living in my doll house I have to laugh." And there was Joe the soldier, and O'Malley the cop. They remained favorite characters even though they were metal and O'Malley's leg was broken off."

It was comforting to leave the here-and-now and allow herself to travel back to enjoy the enduring remnants from a happier, innocent time.

"I'm sorry. For a moment I became transported. You always knew how to make me laugh. I can visualize you entertaining our sister. Jeremy, you've always had such an imagination. No wonder you became a teacher. You still know how to gather the young. Please, continue," she encouraged.

Jeremy returned to the present but seemed distracted. He foraged into his pocket and produced a cigarette. "I'll be back in a few minutes." Another eccentric habit, and this time she stuck with her "eccentric" word. No one ever could figure it out. It being why Jeremy always excused himself to smoke. Was he being considerate to those who didn't smoke? Or, maybe, he connected "time out" with cigarettes. No matter. He soon returned to their table and seemed prepared to conclude the revelation of events imposed upon him.

"The truth is I don't know what happened...really...I mean why Rita died. All I'm able to resurrect from my infantile portrayal is that I must have gotten lost in some project and didn't notice Rita leaving the room. That is, until the scream."

"The scream. What scream?"

"The scream? The scream that turned my blood to ice and shattered my childhood in an instant. By the time I started to breathe again and followed the sound to the kitchen I knew who screamed. Mother was kneeling on the floor in front of the kitchen sink with Rita in her arms. You know those scenes where people are moving in slow motion and their lips are moving without sound?" My five year old brain had to be swirling! When everything fell back into place and slowed down, it appeared to me dad was moving quickly... like darting in rapid motion. It could have been that my feet were glued in place.

"This is when, I recall, I felt a nudge from behind me. It was Charles attempting to move me out of my petrified state. When I looked around he was beckoning. I guess I followed him out of the room because I brushed by a form in the doorway. My dreams always had that person in the doorway and Charles silent in the shadows motioning me to follow."

Jeremy suddenly stood up. He stretched and then turned to beckon to the waiter. After ordering refills on the coffee for both, he adjusted his position in the seat and continued.

"Yes, I had dreams for a long time. I haven't thought about the scream for years. It used to wake me from a sound sleep. The form in the doorway was always part of the dream before waking, and I figured it out eventually. Nobody talked much about that night and Charles always cautioned me not to bring it up. The form was dad holding the door for me ...like offering me an escape route. One night I must have walked through the door for the last time and the dreams stopped. A counselor helped me understand years later that dad was most likely offering me an instant exit from guilt and a lifetime of remorse. It took years before I gave myself permission to accept it, probably at his funeral. And I never looked back again. That is, until now."

Liz felt warm tears burning her eyes. However, her brother's tragic narrative kept her fixed upon his every word, at the same time rummaging in her pockets for a Kleenex. Without warning her response tumbled out of control. She began repeating over and over, filling up the space left by her brother's abrupt closure.

"I'm sorry. I'm sorry. I'm so sorry. I opened all of that up again, And now...and now," she repeated," I have to respond. I'm committed to seeing this through, and that to me means, sifting out the pain you may be feeling, along with beginning to unravel the pieces of my own life that you've churned up at my insistence."

Liz was startled when Jeremy reached over the table and cupped her free hand in his.

"I have to tell you something, So, blow your nose and listen. Here, take a sip of coffee. Please, Liz. Don't feel bad. I'm not feeling pain. I thought I would but I don't! Sadness, maybe. But, at the same time, I'm grateful. Sad for losses, yes, but grateful that we can sit here scratching at old wounds and neither of us disintegrated. Me, especially. I just recalled the worst night of my life and it didn't destroy me. Had you not brought all of this to the surface, I wouldn't know what I know now. It didn't hurt. I don't hurt anymore. Isn't that amazing?"

Jeremy stood up to leave, gathered extra napkins from the register counter and handed them to Liz. "Come on, let's walk." Liz increased her pace to keep up with him. The air felt warm and soothing. They boarded the bus without words. As they stepped off the bus and began to walk along the gated gardens at Tudor City Jeremy spoke "Let's sit on a bench." It was dusk and the gardens were mellowing in the light of a full moon just beginning to rise over the East River.

Jeremy slid onto a bench and sighed. His lean frame stretched out and he leaned his head back.

"So," he began, "you understand now that I don't know what happened the night Rita died. Or maybe she didn't die that night. It was mentioned she was taken to the hospital. Does it really matter? What mattered was that she died and nothing was ever the same after that. Mother became distant, that is, except from Charles. Dad? He would sometimes lift me on his lap and just talk...ramble. A therapist helped me understand this bond I was experiencing with dad. It was built on sharing the guilt But, whatever it was, it filled the emptiness that Rita's passing left. And'...he repeated...'and you, Little Lizzie, were born a few months later."

Precious Lizzie!

"Yep, I was precious alright. Our daddy thought the sun rose and set on me. And Charles was Mother's Knight You, my brother was "lost child," huh? Oh, that really hurts!"

"And that's what I want you to understand. I don't hurt anymore!" What was that song dad used to sing to you?" Jeremy's question broke through her thoughts and called her out of sadness to respond,

"The song? Oh, yes, the song he used to sing to me...it was "Daddy's Little Girl." I tear up whenever I hear that...and right now I'm drowning." Liz let her thoughts rest. After moments of stillness her attention moved to memories of her dad sitting across from her at the dinner table.

She hummed and the words came. Her brother listened as she sang softly, "You're the end of the rainbow, my pot of gold," the words and melody rose and then faded out with "You're sugar and spice and everything nice,..." and Jeremy joined in, "and you're daddy's little girl!"

A movement of light overhead joined their duet's finale. Liz sat up and searched its location. "Did you see the shooting star?" she asked. "It just flashed across the sky."

Jeremy remained disenchanted. "So?" he commented. Undaunted, she explained, "Remember how Mother and Daddy used to harmonize? We sang at gatherings, on Sunday drives, or on the spur of the moment when daddy would mellow and suddenly begin singing some of his favorites. Mother would always join in. It was good to listen and observe them when they sang together.

They seemed to come together again and enjoy one another. Ignoring her brother's obvious lack of engagement, Liz summed it up. "I believe there is something or someone bigger than us, a life force, a benevolent intelligence, whatever one recognizes and names, that holds us together. Like the universe," she continued. And nature... humans, "all one dynamic whole," as Chardin wrote. She relaxed against the back of the bench and gazed up. I think the same life force that holds those stars in place is also holding us together. I think, Mother and Daddy are together, and hitched a ride on that star that crossed overhead when they heard us singing."

His response was a long time in coming. "Dreamer." "Yes, and isn't it fun?" she replied. They had covered enough. They had filled another day. Liz rose and headed for the gate. "You go up and I'll follow you shortly."

Liz turned to see him searching in his jacket for a cigarette. He looked at her and smiled.

"I'm fine," he assured her and relaxed against the bench with his head tilted back. She turned to leave but paused as she considered his parting comment. "I'll join you shortly. I just need a little time to reflect." She waited and he added, "Who knows. Maybe if I stay and watch, I'll catch mother and dad staging another flyover."

Liz was unprepared. She rebounded on a happy thought. "Who knows?" She stood in place for a moment and let her imagination form a comeback. "But, if you're not up in a half hour I'll suspect you hitched a ride." She contorted her face into a frown and puckered her lips. "I'll miss you."

Chapter 16

No Task, No Tears
Little bird on your feet
stunned, still, waiting.
Eyes filmed to focus
beyond my sight to grasp.
Time seems enough for you,
dying not a task.

Little bird, messenger of hope,
who sent you to my window today
to while away your dying?
Creatures of the same fate are we,
only you say goodbye without crying.

Noble creature,
silent teacher,
you know.
I mind you.

Liz opened the newspaper and realized she had lived through a whole year without a sense of any real time. The date registering 2004 pulled her out of a constant lethargy plaguing her since her return to the Midwest from the last of a series of trips to Coral Gables, Florida.

She sighed. She'd been sighing lately, deep sighs, resounding from someplace she wasn't sure. But they seem to physically lift her heart and "sort of reposition it," she thought. It was only at these times when she sighed, that she became aware of her heart. Lately it seemed to be weighted, listless, pulling energy from her. She tried absorbing the Minutes of the staff meeting but it took too much effort. She slid the paper to the back of her desk and tilted her chair back. Without reason she found herself studying the ceiling. Following the lines of the cobweb directly over her desk reminded her that winter was ready to concede its grip in exchange for fresh air and spring cleaning. With that thoughtless observation she sighed and forced herself to return to her mail.

Jeremy didn't hitch a ride on a passing star that night at Tudor Greens. It was three years later, in March of 2004, that her "sugar daddy brother yielded to the inevitable after a six-month battle with pancreatic cancer. Liz remembered those series of phone conversations that left her unsettled. "You sound like you may need someone to sort and organize. Are you inviting me to visit you in Florida?" "Yeah," his answer came in slow exhale, she had noted, best described as relief. "Yes, that would be great, sister. Lately, I'm realizing how fast things pile up if you don't keep at them...like paperwork, bills..." and after a thoughtful silence, he added, "It's been suggested by co-workers that I simply start getting rid of accumulation, and maybe I could start with my office. I am ready to concede. It's either that or take the coward's way and move...and, by that I mean, out of the country."

Liz's thoughts became confused. The contents and tone of their conversations of late unsettled her. "Well, brother, as much as I can figure at this distance, you may need an objective eye to pierce through your compulsive clutter. And, if you need someone to add affirmation to your tendency for procrastination, I'm just that person. This said, I am only too happy to accept your invitation. Then, of course, when you have been restored to an ordered life, and I, hopefully, have a gorgeous suntan, we can follow up with black markers and sticky labels. Between breaks, if I recall, we will visit your friends for guitar sessions and singalongs, not to mention sharing your preference for fancy restaurants. I have just one request? Can we fill the empty spaces around the beer in your refrigerator with something more substantial...like food?"

Jeremy's groan interrupted her attempts to override the dread that was beginning to lurk on the edges of her thoughts. "There you go again...conditions, conditions, conditions!"

Hearing his light comeback, she continued. "And maybe you could test to see if the stove still works. Another skill of mine is cooking. If I stay long enough, you may learn to boil water and who knows what your future holds after that discovery!"

Jeremy picked her up at the airport two weeks later. As she had busied herself planning her trip. her initial feelings of dread intensified. They hadn't seen one another since his visit in the fall. "What if's" had her reeling. "What if he's seriously ill? What if I have to stay with him? What if I find I can't override my fear of sickness, hospitals and...God forbid.. body contact with the dying! Jen could do it. She's a hospice nurse. She would dive right in, like Mother Theresa. What if...." Her frantic reliance on denial became more apparent with each day as she fought for calm and to keep focused. "Why did I think I could avoid my own fears forever? Life eventually hits us front and center. Truth is good for us. Right? What a wimp you are Liz! You're the one that's scratching the dirt off layers of family secrets and now you wince at meeting your own ghosts face to face!"

Normally on planes she welcomed the pilot's announcement of descent and landing. This time, however, the sound of the engines reversing conjured up an image of herself hung on a trapeze waiting to be lifted out of a freefall. Her moment of truth awaited her on the tarmac. Fear leaped from the shadows and flooded her whole being with sadness so unexplainably heavy, she had to force herself to rise from her seat. The crowds and noise of the terminal as she waited at baggage claim brought more agitation.

The Florida air tickled her nose. The humidity, as she walked out, always seemed different than that of Minnesota. "Like feathers, it wafted lightly upon the senses, as opposed to the heaviness we endure in the north country." A flash of grey diverted her attention as a car slowed in front of her and Jeremy's head tilted into the sunlight glancing off the driver's window. In the past the door would fly open and his leg would follow simultaneously. This time she waited. As Jeremy stepped out of his car and greeted her his appearance jolted her into a full stop, like a sudden shattering impact with the wall that had protected her from reality. Oh, she remembered praying in that moment "that her face did not register the agony that tore into her at having her worst fears confirmed." Jeremy was very ill.

March flew by in a spiral of funeral arrangements, meetings with bankers, lawyers, and the grieving friends, gathering family from different parts of the country, as well as arranging lodging for everyone. Once fearful at the aspect, she returned overwhelmed, not only by her own strength when challenged, but by the outpouring of care and assistance from persons, some whom she was meeting for the first time. Trust was non-negotiable in the time frame allowed to her. Her response to organizing chaos proved to be the most demanding. She drew from hidden resources of mind, body and spirit. She arrived home exhausted. But, on her first night back, truth sparked a brief moment of self-admiration. "Lizzy," she said to herself, "who is this woman? Is she the same one you have habitually called "Wimp"?" "You betcha," she whispered into her pillow, sighed and let exhaustion carry her into tender oblivion.

Now, only a month later, she was still processing the rapid chain of events that left her groping through a fatigue and sadness that seemed incurable. Even so, April temperatures were beginning to stir up the garden outside St. Joseph's. The crocuses had peeked through and were starting to bud. Liz attention was suddenly averted from the crocuses by a darting movement outside her window, accompanied by a crushing sound. Something... a bird...had flown into the window by her desk. Startled, she moved away and then reversed her chair forward. Ever since Jeremy's death, she had been drawn into these bouts of brooding reflection until like now, she was jarred out by a sudden interruption. She swiveled her chair into position and leaned forward, captivated in the face of a tiny bird looking directly at her from the ledge outside. Its feathers moved as it labored to breathe.

Instantly her attention was drawn away from the notes on her desk, to an event more significant in its unfolding. She sat in silence, watching, waiting. Momentary concerns faded and time was brought to sacred pause. The clock ticked, and Liz could hear the sound of her own breathing as she settled into a death watch with nature.

She skipped coffee break and lunch. Instead, with the afternoon sun positioned over them, she scooped out a grave in the soft moist soil with the only tool she could find... a Panera plastic spoon, and laid the fragile form gently into the ground. "You lived with dignity and died with dignity." Reacting to a flippancy she heard in her tone, undoubtedly brought on by the anger of grief, she added, "Maybe we'll see each other again." Still, her blessing appeared trite and apologetic. She continued undaunted. "May you return to our Creator, gentle friend, and receive the fullness of joy Jesus promises to all of us, Amen." Satisfied she had given her friend a proper burial, Liz looked about to make sure no one was watching her strange ritual by the flower beds. Assured and momentarily consoled by her dedication to the dying, she made her way inside.

In her ministry Liz was familiar with funerals. She had prepared many families "to say farewell to a loved one" as the print stated in the brochures. As events reeled about her after Jeremy's first call, the problem became tragically clear as the months passed. Pain and panic engulfed her as she lay the phone down that day seven months ago. As much as she remembered, she had stared blankly, her mind drawn into emptiness, before consciousness slowly returned. All of her experience ministering to families of the grieving did not prepare her for the dread that refused to leave her that morning when her brother asked her to visit him in Florida. It was the slightest of tremor in his voice, the pauses in his speech.

"You didn't show for coffee, so I brought you a cup." It was Anne whose hand extended from behind the door Liz had left ajar. She held out a cup she had managed to slip through the space. Liz refocused on the image of her friend paused now in the doorway. Anne, dear Anne. She had gone through gastric bypass during Liz's leave to be with Jeremy. Her smile radiated from a slim, stylishly dressed figure.

To finish off the transformation, Liz noted, she had even added a blond highlight to her hair. "Bless you, Miss Gorgeous," she quipped reaching for the coffee! "The elixir of the gods...and, I read, also the preferred brew of pilots everywhere. The fuel that runs the social engines of the world You are a jewel!" Noting a look of concern on Anne's face, Liz changed her tone. "What? What's wrong?"

Their relationship had grown into a comfortable familiarity over the years. "What's that?" Liz asked as a box, labeled in fine print, which she was no longer able to read at first glance, was placed on her desk. "Rice crackers." Seeing the raised eyes, Anne assured her, "They're delicious. Try one."

"They come with a personal guarantee, huh. I've been meaning to tell you how much I enjoyed our lunches together before you gave up pastas and dairy fats." Liz smiled as the rice crunched between her teeth. "Not bad," but she couldn't resist raising her hand to shield herself from Anne's "tolja'so" smile. "But, not totally good." And then reconsidered, "However, the crunch does make a happy sound. That is definitely a plus and encourages further testing." She foraged into the box again and leaned back into her chair with her coffee. "So, did I miss anything at the lunch session?"

Anne smiled again, like she were about to deliver the news of a pay raise. "We missed you." Switching subjects, her voice came through with this subtle note of apology, as if she had ventured into something without permission and wasn't sure of what Liz's reaction would be. "The phone rang during lunch and as I was standing by the window in conversation, I noticed you in the garden. You have to understand from my vantage point it was a strange scene to behold. Being a farm girl I knew it was too late for bulbs and too early for planting. So what on earth could she be doing," I said to myself. "Ah, so that's what caused the troubled look," Liz thought to herself.

"There she was again, Anne of Sunny Brook Farm, calm, respectfully inquisitive, encouraging trust with what Liz had begun to call, "soft humor." She struggled defining an image. Aha! Similar, maybe, to the teacher communicating their shared humanness to a child who was caught wearing his sister's dresses. "I know you have an explanation for this. Just tell Annie everything and we'll talk about it, Precious." "Well, of course," it dawned! "It's a skill taught and honed through practice. Anne is a teacher! A Youth Education Director!" Liz looked over and sipped from her cup. Anne broke the silence, Liz reminded her later, "with a "titch of growing impatience." "Are you going to tell me," she asked, "or are you going to leave me hanging. That would be very painful because right now !"

Liz interrupted, "I was digging a grave." She watched Anne's eyes focus with new interest. Liz continued, "No, if you noticed the size of the plastic spoon I was wielding, you will believe me when I say I was burying a bird. And no, again. In my current bereavement I have not developed a grave fetish." Liz was biding time to decide how to share something so unexplainable even to herself. "He and I..." she started, "...the bird... shared a sacred time together and when his spirit finally departed ...I...," Liz struggled as she chose words to describe the bird's eyes as life faded behind a luminous film and the lightness of his little body, almost brittle in the warm breeze."

Anne broke through suddenly. "You mean while we were having coffee, you were sitting watching a bird die?"

"Weird, huh? Although, maybe, not the weirdest in our professions."

Anne interrupted, "Why? What was the fascination?"

Liz's brain clicked and she looked gratefully at her friend. "Because I wasn't there when Jeremy died." There it was. Her words brought form to all the feelings she'd been wrestling down since the first day of her arrival home. Now she was able to understand the gratitude she felt for Anne's inquiry.

"I had returned to Minnesota just hours before his passing," she continued. "It explains that heart rendering sadness when I was told the next morning Jeremy had left...didn't even hang in for another visit. Spending time with Jeremy dying; sharing those last moments was a need I was not even aware of...until today. A need that I didn't understand but felt it gnawing at me these past weeks." Liz rose and walked to the window. "You see, I didn't sit with Jeremy during those last hours. I didn't help him on his way. I felt cheated! I shared his illness, his depression, his anger as he struggled, all the preparations for death, everything! But never got to see him leave...to send him off. Just now it came to me, so clear, so kind, so forgiving.

Strange how self-revelation brings with it absolution...like, "The truth will set you free." Liz looked at her friend and felt a buoyancy in her heart, the heart that had languished for weeks. "Thank you. You helped." She turned towards Anne and stepped forward to emphasize her next statement. "Suddenly, it became so clear! This little bird gave me the experience of death that would prepare me to go on living." Liz heard her voice rising. " Without that, I was denied the peace and the beauty, the Presence that people have described in those last moments. Isn't it weird when you expect life to make sense? Like today, I was invited to share the experience with a bird. And in return, burying that little bird was my way of honoring the gift that sweet little creature gave to me during his last moments." Liz reached for her chair and folded into it. Her words muffled as she bowed her head into her hands and wept softly. Liz felt Anne guiding her to her feet. She didn't resist Anne's embrace but nestled into the comforting warmth of her friend's arms. What a gift, to meet a person so different than you, and yet, who understands and is able to share the simple and profound experiences of her grief and "Jeremy's bird."

Chapter 17

Empty spaces
empty words.
Nothing places.
Nothing stays
the same for long.

What is lasting
What is treasured?
Why does something
take so long?

Liz opened her eyes and the sound of a tune playing on her cell phone drifted in. "Phone, phone, phone," she repeated through the fog. "Ah!" As she shifted to listening mode she hoped she was up to the caller's obvious enthusiasm. With full knowledge she wasn't, she made an attempt. It was like fighting through smog. "Hi! What time is it? It was Laura, her friend, an extrovert high on the charts. "Guess what?" she asked. "I can't guess anything. I'm hardly awake. Why don't you make it easy and tell me." Encouraged, Laura launched into an account of her latest dilemma. "Julie asked me to puppy-sit. I knew when they got that puppy with their schedules and the time and attention that a puppy needs that...."

Liz endured the first part of her account and interrupted. "I'll call you back, okay?" "I know what you are going to say. You looked forward to your retirement, just decorated your apartment, was looking forward to volunteering at the Community Theatre..." Laura countered by breaking in. "Yes, you know how we looked forward to this time in our lives." Promising to speak with her after she became coherent, Liz put down her phone and hurried in the direction of her coffee maker which had begun making happy perking sounds in the background of conversation.

"Poor Laura. She looked forward to this time to enjoy her retirement. And here I am looking forward to a reunion with family in Minnesota. She sipped her coffee and surveyed the early risers walking to their jobs at the United Nations. Listened to the growing rumble of traffic buildup and chuckled when she heard the neighbor dogs greeting one another, and thought of Laura's dilemma. "It seems we are always looking forward to life instead of fully living in it. Contentment is a word so seldom used unless to describe a moment rather than a time frame. What are we looking forward to? Perhaps it would be different with each person we ask. Am I content? Or have I been just using this time to delve and decipher so that I, too, can move on? Interesting," Liz answered herself as she refilled her coffee cup. "Wake up, Liz, and greet the day!" The first sip of her refill lay on her tongue when clarity came upon her with force. "The day! Oh, my gosh," she gulped, "today I am supposed to check in for my boarding pass! I leave for Minnesota in the morning!"

Minnesota and its memories filled her thoughts as she packed the last of her clothes for two weeks in "the north country" as her father used to reference her new residency. She sighed when contemplating leaving her down comforter. "It doesn't take long to become attached to comforts...and comforters. She sat on her bed and let her hand graze over the top of the bed cover. "We wrap ourselves in the familiar and some like myself, so snug, I have to be coaxed out like a bear in January. Travel and change suits the young much better.

Travel never used to bother her. Every Spring, and ever since her first experience of air travel, Liz would feel that urge to experience life again at thirty thousand feet, never losing the awe that came watching the thick cotton cloud formations so close they seemed to glance off the window, so high they appeared like snow-covered mountain tops, and then, there was always the added thrill of the destination. At the age of twenty three, following her marriage, when she informed her parents she would be moving to Minnesota, her father had warned "be prepared for frigid cold and grueling winters!" Ironically, that winter of her arrival in Minnesota back in 1957, New York was hit with a rare winter blast. There are pictures stored away showing cars buried in white and snowdrifts reaching halfway up the doorways of buildings. It didn't take her long to settle in. Her first experience of Midwestern hospitality was of exiting the terminal and encountering a pheasant walking proud along the curb, looking like a "plant" from the Chamber of Commerce.

Displaced newlyweds, he from Glenwood, Minnesota, she from the Bronx in New York, they rented a little apartment on the top floor of a farm house in the rural outskirts of Madison, Wisconsin close to her husband's new work assignment. It was here that Liz had her first encounter with "rural folk." And the town complete with a one-room school house. In the Fall, on the first day of deer hunting opener, the only man left in town was the grocer. It took years for her to understand the excitement in every hunter to "bag the Big Buck," gut it, drag it out, and appear on the freeway with his trophy strapped to the top of his vehicle.

Learning to swim in fresh water was another adjustment for a girl growing up on the beaches on the east coast buoyed up by the salt in the ocean waters. In a succession of first experiences, Liz decided some were better left to ignorance, such as hunting. Specifically, the sport of pheasant hunting which, along with firearms, required an athletic stamina to master the demands of plodding through a slough. A slough goes on for acres and has mounds of deep rows of mud and weeds...high weeds...thick weeds, sometimes dry, crispy weeds. Pheasants nest in them and, of course have the skill of flying by which they gracefully extricate themselves. When one is a ground creature only five feet, six inches tall, walking through these and over the mounds, this requires lifting your knees high with each step. It's similar to a show horse in "high gait" until the leg muscles begin to ache under the stress Liz, sizing up the toll it took on her, vowed never again to inflict such agony upon herself just to accommodate another's folly.

After walking over swampy mounds well into the morning, Liz was unable to keep up with the hunters. Reaching her limit, she fell to her knees to rest. That's when she spotted the high ground encircling the field and decided to watch the hunters from the top of the hill. On her knees, and through the high grass thick on the hillside, she began her ascent. A few moments into her trek she heard the sounds of gun fire and heard shouts of "keep going, Liz!" It was only when she reached her destination and looked down on the scene below that it became clear to her. And this was she had flushed more birds in those few moments than the dogs had the entire morning!

The Midwest was a grand place to raise children, and pets, grow vegetables, enjoy camping, dining around the fires at night on the fresh catch of the day, There were open fields, crystal lakes, expanses of fresh virgin snow for snowmobiling and ice skating rinks right in our back yards after moving to a home on the lake.

And, so, why New York? Yes, Liz remembers the day she was informed that Jeremy had left his apartment to her in his will. It didn't take but a few solo trips for her to become lured into moving. "Deep within me I felt this awakening, this call to live out Jeremy's plan to become a resident of Manhattan. Time affirmed her move. Understanding grew slowly, that of a link with her own deep yearnings for completeness. She discovered the reliving of childhood events along with continuing to revisit places from her past, expanded her sense of time and awareness into fresh observations. "It was like reviewing a movie and being pulled deeper into what was overlooked in the previous showing."

Sitting now, many years later, reflecting in the quiet, Liz became aware of the peace she had always enjoyed in her bed room. Simultaneously, her mind quickened as if someone opened a window to let in fresh air. Family pictures on the wall by her bed caught her attention. As well as something she had never noticed before. There were only two photos that plainly revealed a sadness not evident in the others. They were of her mother and the other of Jeremy. "The Woman of

Many Sorrows" and the "Lost Boy," she repeated, struck by the discovery. The realization brought a flashback of the night in Tudor Gardens. It was that night Jeremy revealed to her the years of struggle after Rita's death, and of his quest for peace through Buddhism, "If I didn't meditate I wouldn't be able to manage life," he told her. Knowing he had found peace and acceptance of himself lifted a burden of worry from her for which she was grateful. Of whatever secrets, whatever fears were released that night, she wasn't fully aware. But as she allowed herself to rest in the memory she could almost hear his voice joining with hers for their duet. Like back then, the joy she felt rose up in her as she allowed the scene to unfold once more. His words when she motioned to leave came back to her, "You go ahead... I just need a little time to reflect," he said, and then added, "Who knows? Maybe I'll catch mother and dad staging another flyover."

That night was the catalyst that brought evidence of her own struggles with their mother. Those long walks through Manhattan over the years slowly encouraged feelings long put in submission, to emerge. She, like Jeremy, also carried a false guilt of childhood feelings of responsibility for the dysfunctions in her family, the slow effects of daily contact, like osmosis. Liz can't pinpoint the timing of her liberation. It was a series of experiences that brought the light-bulb moment. She was led to read Irish history. She was enlightened by the description of the rituals of the Irish to express their grief. During these readings, and learning of the plight of the first immigrants from Ireland in the early 1900's she began to suspect her mother grew up in a steady environment of death rituals and sorrow. The fact that her mother was one of nine siblings of whom only three survived added further credence. She grew up with her Aunt Edna and Uncle Ray. There were great losses suffered by families in the early 1900's. Her own memories growing up were of how little was shared about the deceased once the time of mourning was over, as if grief was packed away with the black clothing. After which, life went on. Was her sister, Rita's death just one too many? As she pondered much later, her mother's grief must have been so prolonged, so great" she concluded, she was unable to celebrate my birth just a few months later.

"It makes sense, after so many losses she rationed herself for the demands another loss might place upon her. Was she afraid to love me? Or just plain and simple emotionally used up. No, I choose to think it was her fear of losing me that caused the distance between us.

Liz rose and lifted her mother's picture from the wall to cradle it in her lap. Her eyes settled once more on the beautiful, sad, brown eyes of her mother looking into hers. How deep was Liz's hunger to delve behind the sadness and discover this woman's character and courage.

She reached for her journal and wrote: "Marion was not only my mother, she was a woman, a daughter, a wife, a person, a woman of great courage and faith who, at the age of sixty, after years of being a homemaker, took the subway to Macy's downtown Manhattan and applied for a sales job! For the next five years she shone in women's wear. Of course, she was always classy. I learned "class" from her...style. My mother was the "dark Irish". Our father used to chide her in fun when she would get angry. "That's the Spanish in you. You have a black heart." And we would all laugh.

My mother was beautiful. My mother was tragic. My mother nurtured, cared for, nursed us, baked delicious cakes and pies, "from scratch," they would say). She served balanced healthy meals long before the emergence of Whole Food chains, set our table with fresh cloth every evening, entertained our friends, washed the team's football uniforms, knitted and sewed with style and skill.

Known to only a few, she kept a secret closet. It contained beautiful dishes, expensive linens, silver sets, and unused treasures she planned to put out for company when my dad bought that house he kept promising her. This is why I know, though unshared, my mother kept planning for a life different from her realities of the cramped space in our little apartment.

My dad went on periodic binges. I am convinced her struggle to keep the secrets of weakness and dysfunction from invading her daily life had a very real and sustaining influence on all of us. For her love, unlike her dreams, was not hidden nor like the grief she feared to share. Her love was strong and transmitted to us in her creation of something beautiful and solid in that small apartment in the Bronx.

Her presence created a home we always returned to. A haven of stability and welcome whether one of us had a scraped knee, a teenage rejection, or returning from two years of active duty. Her commitment to making sense out of life as it was, and not succumbing to fearful fantasy, kept our family demons away from us and kept my father sober."

Liz finished writing and looked up. "To be continued," she whispered. Her family seemed to be smiling from the wall. Liz found herself smiling back. She found the next moment so joyful, and amusing. "I might be going crazy," she said to herself, "but it feels so good!" She became silent collecting the few remaining thoughts before moving from the bed. "Love..." She paused and moved on, "When we love, our presence is not diminished by distance, nor even by death. It grows stronger as the next generation seeks and draws from us the strength for their own lives. My life is not perfect, but even in its imperfections, it is a gift I give freely."

Still smiling now at her mother's photo in her lap, she dialed Clare in Minnesota. "Hi! It's me!" She heard Clare's warm response, "Is this my mother?" Liz laughed, "Yes, this is your mother. I'm arriving tomorrow, remember? And about that question you ask every year...I am going to think about moving back. Yes! Back to Minnesota! We'll talk further when I'm there. Oh," Liz sighed, "so many stories...so much to share. Oh, yes, and, tell Jen I can't wait to see her."